Mira

Mira

The Divine Lover

V. K. Sethi

Radha Soami Satsang Beas

Published by:
J. C. Sethi, Secretary
Radha Soami Satsang Beas
Dera Baba Jaimal Singh
Punjab 143 204, India

Fourth edition 2009

16 15 14 13 12 11 10 09   8 7 6 5 4 3 2 1

ISBN 978-81-8256-832-7

Printed in India by: Lakshmi Offset Printers

Contents

PART I
Life and Message

PART II
Selected Poems

PREFACE

Mira, the Divine Lover, another title in the Mystics of the East Series, presents the life and message of one of the most popular devotees that India has produced. Born and brought up in a royal family, Mira followed the path of divine love with unflinching dedication, in spite of public censure, persecution by her family and even attempts on her life.

Love and devotion for the Lord and the Master come alive for us in the songs of Mira. Her personal story of love and longing for God, exquisitely expressed in her inimitable poems, has been sung in Indian households for hundreds of years. Men and women, young and old, have sung her songs at village weddings, at village wells and in the streets. Mira expresses her longing for the Lord and the pain of separation from her Master with the anguish of a bride torn from her bridegroom. What she sings of is what all devotees sing of, deep within their heart. It is a cry to end duality, to merge in the One, to live in eternal and lasting bliss and peace. It is a song that is the same today as it was when Mira was singing. It is the song of love.

The poems selected for this volume are presumed to be those composed after Mira came in contact with Saint Ravidas. The poems clearly reflect the unity of the message of all mystics, who always urge us to seek the Lord within the temple of our own body, to learn the technique of going within ourselves from a true Master, and through the practice of Shabd or Nam, imparted by the Master, to journey into the inner regions and reach our True Home.

S. L. Sondhi
Secretary

Radha Soami Satsang Beas
April, 1979

PART I

Life and Message

Mira's Life

The impact of Mira's personality and character was not felt by her contemporaries in its full measure. She was looked upon as a disgrace to the royal family in which she was married, and early chroniclers of Rajasthan, her home state in northwest India, have referred to her name casually. The bards who eulogized the valour and exploits of kings and warriors did not bother to mention Mira in their songs. Though connected with two powerful ruling houses of Rajasthan—Merta by birth and Mewar through marriage—historically she remained in the background, perhaps destined to be forgotten.

Mira, however, could not be easily forgotten. Her devotion, her faith and firmness, her life of one-pointed dedication to the Lord, have left an indelible mark on the path of time. In the cultural life of the country she has remained shining through the past 450 years, a star with an ever-increasing brilliance. Ignored by historians, she lived in the hearts of the people through her lyrical compositions—compositions whose appeal and popularity have remained undiminished. Many of Mira's celebrated contemporaries now live only in the pages of history, but Mira with time has grown in stature as the most dynamic, inspiring and loved devotee and poet of her era.

Many modern scholars have conducted research on the life of Mira, but almost all of them admit that nothing can be said with certainty about the details of her life. The main sources of information about Mira's life are: (1) her own autobiographical poems, (2) the poetical works of later devotees, and (3) the deductions drawn by various scholars during the last 150 years based on known historical events.

(1) Mira's poems were spontaneous outbursts of her emotions; they were sung and recited, but there is no record to show that they were put into writing during her lifetime. Many collections of her poems are available in manuscript form in state and private collections in Rajasthan and Gujarat. These poems, however, were compiled and written fifty to one hundred years after Mira's death. (2) The accounts of later devotees deal only with miracles associated with Mira's life and fail to give chronological details. (3) The deductions of history mostly run along the slim edge of surmise and speculation.

Thus the story of Mira's life available to us today is based on traditions and legends of Mira, which modern scholars have attempted to put into the framework of history.

Mira was born in 1498 in the town of Kudki (Bajoli according to some scholars). She was the daughter of Ratan Singh and the granddaughter of Rao Duda, the ruler of Merta, an independent and powerful state in Rajasthan. Her father, being one of the younger sons of Rao Duda, was the chief of only twelve small towns and villages near Merta. When Mira was barely two years old, her mother died and Rao Duda, the grandfather, brought the child Mira to Merta, where she grew up under the veteran warrior's loving guardianship.

Rao Duda was a man with a devotional bent of mind, and holy men were regular visitors to his palace. Mira thus came in contact with holy men from her childhood, and her spiritual tendencies developed from an early age.

As was customary in the royal families, Mira's education included knowledge of scriptures, music, spinning and sewing, along with archery, fencing, horse riding and driving chariots. Thus she was trained to carry out domestic chores in the household, and to wield weapons in case of war. Mira made good progress in both fields. Her learning gave her a broad outlook and her military training gave her courage, firmness and determination. She was soft-spoken, mild-mannered and gifted with a sweet and melodious voice. Affectionate, kind and charitable by disposition, she was reputed to be one of the most extraordinary beauties of her time.

Learning of her qualities, Rana Sangram Singh, more commonly known as Rana Sanga, the powerful King of Mewar, personally approached Mira's grandfather for her hand in marriage for his eldest son and heir, Prince Bhojraj. The engagement ceremony was carried out with great rejoicing both at Chittor, the capital fort of Mewar, and at Merta. But Rao Duda, who had brought up Mira as his own child and who was both father and mother to her, did not live to see the marriage. He passed away a few months after the engagement. Mira deeply loved her grandfather, and this was the first shock received in her life.

Mira's uncle, her father's elder brother Rao Viram Dev, who was also very fond of her, arranged her marriage and gave away the bride in 1516. Mira was then eighteen years old. The marriage was performed with great pomp and show; the entire city of Merta was decorated like a bride. Rana Sanga, who came with the marriage party accompanied by many rulers and chiefs, was very happy with the match, for he had found a beautiful and accomplished daughter-in-law in Mira, who was ideally suited to be the future queen of Mewar. At the time of her marriage, Mira was given a number of villages, besides jewellery and clothes, by her uncle Rao Viram Dev. Rana Sanga received his daughter-in-law with great affection, and along with gifts of ornaments and finery he allotted the revenue of a large number of villages to Mira.*

Prince Bhojraj, Mira's husband, was a handsome young man who had already earned a name as a warrior. Mira, it is generally presumed, had a happy married life and was well looked after in the house of her in-laws. But this happiness proved to be short-lived—Prince Bhojraj died in a battle in 1525–26, about ten years after the marriage.† It must have been a great shock to Mira. Rana Sanga had selected her to be the future queen of Mewar, but fate had destined otherwise.

Six months after the death of her husband, Mira faced two more jolts. Her father Ratan Singh died in 1527, fighting on Rana Sanga's side against Babur in the battle of Khanua.‡ And Rana Sanga, who had almost taken the place of Rao Duda in Mira's life, sustained wounds in the battle and within a few months was fatally poisoned by some courtiers who intrigued against him.

Mira was greatly shaken by this sudden turn of events. She realized the transient nature of the world. Her inborn devotional tendencies now came to the fore and her thoughts turned inwards. Some of her poems seem to reflect her mood of detachment: "Life in this world is short; why involve yourself in it? The body is false, all material objects are false, false is the entire creation."[1]

---

*According to the inquiries of P. Harinarayan Sharma of Jaipur, the revenue allotted to Mira amounted to 300,000 rupees per year (*Mira Bharat Padavali*, Pt. I, p.v.). It is believed that Mira enjoyed this revenue as long as she lived in Mewar and that she used to spend most of it on feeding devotees and helping the needy.

† According to some scholars Prince Bhojraj died about six years after the marriage in 1522.

‡ The Battle of Khanua was the second in the series of three major battles which gave the Mughal warlord Babur dominion over northern India.

In childhood and early youth Mira was a devotee of Lord Krishna, the incarnation of Lord Vishnu.* Her childhood love for Lord Krishna had by now grown and become mature. She now identified her deity with the one Supreme Being, the everlasting Lord of all.

Sometime in Mira's life an event of great importance took place that brought about a radical change in her entire spiritual outlook. She came in contact with Sant Ravidas, the cobbler Saint, and was initiated by him into the path of Shabd Yoga. With the Master's grace, her inherent devotional bent of mind was given a new direction. Her vision now expanded as her love for the Divine Being became a reality and a profound experience. External observances and formalities, rites and rituals, which had formed a part of her life since childhood, gradually lost their significance.

Scholars differ about the identity of Mira's Master. Nabhadas, in *Bhaktamal*, his book on the lives of holy men, has described Ravidas as a disciple of Ramanand (1299–1417).† There is only one short stanza that enumerates the names of twelve main disciples of Ramanand, Ravidas being one of them. On the basis of this stanza, scholars have said that Ravidas lived between the latter half of the fourteenth and the first half of the fifteenth century, and have rejected the theory that Ravidas was the Master of Mira. But the same stanza of Nabhadas gives the names of some other disciples of Ramanand who, according to modern scholars, were not contemporaries of Ramanand. Sant Mat traditions maintain that Sant Ravidas, also known as

---

*One of the gods in the Hindu triad: Brahma the creator, Vishnu the sustainer and Shiva the destroyer.

†There is considerable difference of opinion about the dates of birth and death of Swami Ramanand, who had a large following throughout northern and western India and is widely believed to have been the Guru of Sant Kabir as well as Sant Ravidas. Various scholars have given his dates as 1328–1448, 1366–1467, 1299–1417, etc.

Raidas, was the disciple of Kabir (1398–1518) and lived to an age of 118 years. According to some traditions Ravidas lived from 1414 to 1532; according to others, from 1434 to 1552.* Research on the life of Ravidas is still being conducted by scholars. Nevertheless, it can be said with certainty that he was a contemporary of Mira for about thirty or forty years of her life, if not more.

The theory propounded by some that Mira had no Master does not stand to reason. Mira has repeatedly pointed out the necessity of a Master in order to realize the Lord. The Saint or Master, according to her, is the doorman to the gates of salvation; he alone holds the key to open the door. With the key of divine love he opens the lock and flings wide the portals of liberation for the soul to enter.[2] She says:

> Without the beloved Lord
> I cannot survive;
> Without the Master,
> At His abode I cannot arrive.[3]

Describing human birth as a rare chance to love and attain the Lord, Mira says the true way to worship the Lord can be obtained only through one who is himself an adept in the ways of devotion. Only such an adept, a true Master, can impart the secret of the path to others. Only he can give us the details of the Inaccessible and His abode.[4]

Mira has mentioned her Master, Ravidas, in some of her poems. In reply to the accusation that she has brought disgrace

---

*Recently, scholars established the birthplace of Sant Ravidas as the small village named Seer Goberdhanpur, situated on the outskirts of Varanasi (formerly Banaras). A memorial to Ravidas was built there in 1971, and it was inaugurated by the Vice-Chancellor of Banaras Hindu University. An old manuscript found at Seer Goberdhanpur gives the dates of Ravidas as 1414–1540.

both to the house of her parents and to that of her husband, she states, "I am no more a denizen of my father's house, nor do I live in that of my husband. I have found my Master in Raidas, and through him the Lord."[5] In another poem she asserts, "I will not give up the practice of Nam that I got from my Master Raidas."[6]

It is only through the grace of Ravidas that Mira could attain her objective:

> I kept searching for the secret
> Of that realm, but none could reveal it.
> When Saint Raidas, my Master, I met,
> He gave my soul the clue to that eternal abode.
> Then I ascended and met my Beloved,
> And my anguish was finally allayed.[7]

> When Raidas, the true Master, I met,
> The severed twig joined again the tree.
> My Master revealed the secret of the Name,
> The flame of Mira merged into the Flame.[8]

Resolved to fulfil the true objective of human birth, namely God-realization, Mira now took to the path of devotion in all earnestness. Her meditation bore fruit and her inner experiences strengthened her convictions and dyed her entire being in the indelible hue of divine love. The spark of love had grown into a glowing flame. In Mira's own words:

> Now my love has taken root and grown,
> Like the tiny seed that grows into an oak.[9]

With the growth of her devotion began a period of trials and tribulations in Mira's life. Her unorthodox approach to God, her unconventional ways of worship, her constant association with holy men, and above all her adoration of her Master, the cobbler Saint Ravidas, were resented by the priestly class and the orthodox people in the court of Chittor. They began to criticize and slander her. The royal family of the Ranas—with their traditional mores, their firm faith in the caste system and the superiority of the higher castes over all others, their conventions of a secluded life for their ladies, and their rigid protocol*—could not brook the thought of one of the ladies of their family associating with commoners, adopting a Master who was a cobbler by profession and low caste by birth, and singing songs in the company of holy men. The priestly class, the orthodox people and the high-caste Brahmins strongly criticized Mira for all this. Exasperated by Mira's total unconcern, they plotted against her and complained to the Rana.

Rana Sanga, who would have sympathized with Mira and understood her suffering, had died in 1527. The new King of Mewar, Rana Ratan Singh, the younger brother of Mira's deceased husband, was weak and impulsive. He lacked the valour, wisdom and tolerance of Sanga, his father. Easily swayed by public opinion, the priests and the court advisers, he looked upon Mira as a blot on the noble house of Mewar. Udabai, a cousin of Prince Bhojraj, took it upon herself to 'reform' her sister-in-law. Some songs by Mira throw light on the attitude of the Rana and Udabai and the firmness of Mira. What taunts and scorn Mira must have suffered at the hands of her sister-in-law and the Rana in her daily life should not be hard to imagine. Udabai nurtured a deep hatred for Mira and did all she could to malign, threaten and torment the devotee of the Lord.

It is said that one night Udabai went to the Rana and told him that there was a man in Mira's room and that she herself

* The protocol of the Ranas of Mewar did not permit them to communicate directly with someone from an inferior caste. Any conversation, when necessary, was conducted through an intermediary.

had heard Mira addressing him in terms of endearment. Mira, in a moment of longing for the Lord, was addressing Him in a state of ecstasy. The Rana, enraged on hearing Uda's report, drew his sword and hurried to Mira's palace, determined to slay her. When he entered the chamber there was no man there. Mira, all alone, was sitting in a state of trance and tears were rolling down her cheeks. A brilliant light emanating from her had completely filled the chamber. As the Rana raised his sword to strike at Mira, he was almost blinded by the light. He rushed out of the room, shaken by the experience.*

Uda, who was waiting outside for the result of the Rana's visit, was surprised at the perplexed expression on her cousin's face as he came out. Unable to understand what had happened, she hurried into the room and was overwhelmed by what she saw. Mira was still sitting, completely oblivious of herself, her face radiant and the room flooded with light. Uda stood spellbound. The realization of her sister-in-law's greatness dawned on her. Struck with deep remorse for trying to bring about Mira's death, she fell at Mira's feet with tears of repentance. Later, the ever kind and forgiving Mira consoled Udabai and took her into her fold.

It is said that the Rana later sent two more ladies to reform Mira, but both of them met with the fate of Uda and became Mira's admirers.

Mira was now deeply immersed in the Lord's love. Praying for His darshan† and longing to meet Him was the sole occupation of her mind. In her own words, she was "staring at the path for Him to come"; her "nights went without sleep"; she "had no

---

* Another version of this story is that the Rana saw dozens of Mira instead of one, in every nook and corner of the chamber.

† Darshan literally means looking at someone. The word, however, does not connote mere looking; it implies looking intently at someone nobler and superior with a deep feeling of respect and devotion and with one-pointed attention.

desire to eat" and "was tossing in anguish like a fish out of water". So deep was Mira's longing for her Beloved that when an astrologer offered to tell her future, she asked him the only question she had on her mind: "Tell me, O good soothsayer, pray tell me when that beloved Lord of mine will I meet?"[10] The astrologer had no answer to give.

There are a number of poems that throw light on the Rana's attempts to compel Mira to change her ways. But Mira's answers to the Rana's harsh words and threats were always dignified and mild:

> Why do you want to kill me, O Rana?
> I have never harmed you,
> Nor have I done any wrong.
> The Lord, in His grace,
> Has given a human body to you,
> And also to me, in order that we worship Him.
> For this gift I gratefully worship Him
> And sing His praises....[11]

> Your considerations of caste and status
> Do not matter to me,
> I only adore the devotees of the Lord....[12]

> Through my Master's power
> And the company of Saints*
> I will swim across the ocean with ease.
> I will drink the precious nectar of Nam,
> Which I have obtained in exchange for my head.[13]

---

* In Sant Mat literature, the term 'Saint' generally refers to a mystic of the highest order, a God-realized mystic who has attained the region of pure spirit. The Hindi term *sant* may also be translated as 'Saint' and have the same meaning, or it may simply denote a holy person.

The actions of the Rana could not shake Mira, nor could the people's slander deter her from following her path. She had cast away all concern for public opinion and knew no fear. She had no thoughts of the world left now, for divine love had completely enveloped her mind, heart and soul.

Mira's association with her Master, it seems, was not a long one. Probably there were only three or four different periods in her life during which she could be with him. Thus most of her life was spent in separation from her beloved Master, which explains the underlying tone of deep sorrow and longing in her poems. Historically, the details of Mira's meeting Sant Ravidas, her initiation and her brief but deeply spiritual association with her Master are not known. What comes down to us in the form of traditions is both inspiring and touching.

Ravidas, during his visits to Chittor, used to live in the colony meant for the people of low caste of those times.* Those of high caste would not visit these colonies nor enter any of the huts. It is believed that at first Mira used to disguise herself in the dress of a low-born maidservant and slip out of her palace to have the darshan of her Master. But through her association with Ravidas, Mira soon realized that the path of Saints is not that of stealth or timidity. Undaunted by any thought of repercussion, she openly started to visit the Saint. She freely sat amongst his common disciples, disregarding their caste and social status; she bowed at the cobbler Saint's feet, adored him and took eatables blessed by him. As long as Ravidas stayed in Chittor, she visited him daily. This is confirmed through one of her poems wherein she is accused of going every morning to the house of the 'low-born one':

---

* In medieval times, people of low caste were permitted to live only in small hutments outside the towns or cities. Some such colonies are still present in parts of Rajasthan. In the city of Mandu, now in ruins, which Ravidas used to visit, his place of residence is still there. It is situated outside the old city of Mandu.

Listen, O Mira, mend your ways.
The Rana forbids you to go,
The family members entreat you
To retrace your steps,
Your friends implore you to desist,
But you do not listen to them.

Sitting in the company of devotees you have
Brought shame and disgrace on yourself.
Every morning you get up and go
To the house of the low-born one
And thus put a blot
On the name of your noble family.[14]

Later, the Rana placed a guard on Mira's section of the palace in order to put a stop to her visits to Ravidas. But nothing could stop Mira. It is believed that she continued to visit her Master by climbing down the steep walls of her palace with the help of a rope made by tying together her *odhhanees* (a scarf-like garment).*

Mira's intense love and devotion for the Master were rewarded with profound inner experiences. She gives some hints of these in her poetry and attributes them to the grace of her Master:

Come to my temple within,
I await Thee, O Lord.
Between the earth and the firmament
Spread glowing colours of dawn
Like torrents of rain.

---

*According to another version, it is said that Mira used to climb down the extremely steep walls of the Chittor Fort itself in the early hours of the morning to visit her Master, Sant Ravidas, who was living in the colony for the low caste outside the Fort.

Through the power of my Master,
I keep repeating the Lord's Name.

Beyond the two planes within,
On the brink of the Lotus of Nam,
I rest with ease.
Beyond the Crooked Tunnel*
Resounds the melody of the flute,
Which I hear through my Master's grace.

My soul, the comely and fortunate bride,
Revels within the township of this body.
The fear of birth and rebirth vanished
When I met a Master, kind and merciful.
Beyond the right and the left,
In the central lane my soul now abides.

It was only when Mira met her Master,
Mighty and powerful,
That she developed true faith and assurance.[15]

Some scholars hold that the Lord Himself was Mira's Master and she did not have a living Master. They have arrived at this conclusion because, like all Saints, Mira identifies her Master with the Lord, since the Master has realized the Lord and become one with Him. Mira's poems expressing her anguish of separation from her Master and her intense longing for him also express the same feelings for the Lord. In many of her lyrics the personality of the Master and the Lord are fused into one. At times she clearly states that God and the Master are one:

---

* *Bunk Nal*, the tunnel between the first and second regions in the soul's inner journey.

> I met the Master
> And through his grace
> I have realized the Truth;
> In my Master I have recognized the Lord....
>
> I have met a Master, primal and eternal;
> Without him I would have continued
> Whirling in the vast ocean of the world.[16]

The hostility of the orthodox people of Mewar kept on increasing. Mira's deep love for the Master further augmented it. But she remained unconcerned and unruffled. People said that she had gone astray, disgraced her family, lost all sense of propriety and gone mad. Mira replies:

> Mad? Yes, I am insane.
> But the love of my Lord
> Through madness I gained....

She continues:

> The bliss for which in vain
> Even gods and angels pray –
> In that bliss this mad one
> Does revel night and day....
>
> People keep branding me
> As mad, time and again;
> But ever the Lord performs
> All tasks of such insane.[17]

Meanwhile, the reign of Rana Ratan Singh was abruptly cut short in the year 1531 when he became a victim of his own intrigue to kill his maternal uncle. The hostile Rana's death, however, did not end Mira's troubles. The new ruler of Mewar, Rana Vikram, was impulsive, self-willed and depraved. Swayed by his orthodox subjects, he soon became a sworn enemy of Mira. In consultation with the priestly class and the city elders, he decided to end Mira's life through poison.

A man named Dayaram was selected to carry the poison in a gold cup and offer it to Mira as *charnaamrit.* Udabai learned of the plot and hurried to warn Mira. But Mira, who had never refused to take *charnaamrit*, gladly drank it though she knew it was poison. After a while, the Rana sent his men to take the body of Mira and throw it in the jungle. But the poison had had no effect on her. They found Mira singing in ecstasy, her face radiant with divine love. In her own words, she came out of the ordeal:

> You gave me poison, O Rana, I know.
> But freed of dross, like gold from the furnace,
> Did Mira emerge pure and beaming bright.[18]

What was the immediate cause that provoked the Rana to take this drastic step against Mira? History and tradition and even legends supply no answer to this question. Nevertheless, it is likely that there was some specific reason that led to this drastic step to get rid of Mira. It is possible that Saint Ravidas was then staying in Chittor or in the vicinity of the fort, and Mira's regular visits to the Saint may have infuriated the priestly class and the royal family to such an extent that they planned her death. In one of her poems Mira says:

---

* *Charnaamrit*, literally 'nectar of the feet', referring to the lotus feet of a Saint or Master, is water or syrup blessed by a Saint or Master; the term is also used for water with which an idol has been washed.

Some evil-minded people saw me
Going daily to the satsang of my Master.
I am happy within myself, for the Lord proved me
True in His judgement, and all the world false.[19]

Mira has mentioned this incident in a number of poems expressing her gratitude to the Lord for "turning the poison into nectar", as she puts it. This incident further increased Mira's love for the Master. She now spent her entire day in devotion and in the company of holy men. Her fame as a devotee started to spread, and people, mostly common folk, began coming to Chittor to listen to her songs of devotion.

It is said that Akbar, the Moghul Emperor, came incognito with Tansen, the great court musician, to have a glimpse of Mira and listen to her inspiring songs. He was overwhelmed by her personality and bowed to her, offering her a precious necklace, which Mira declined to accept. Historically, this incident could not have taken place when Mira was in Chittor, for Akbar ascended to the throne in 1556 when Mira had already left Chittor. Hermann Goetz, in his biography of Mira, maintains that Akbar visited Mira at a much later date, in Amer,* where she lived for a time during her later life. The impact of her personality must have left a deep impression on the mind of young Akbar, who later developed a broad outlook and tried to find a religion of universal acceptability.

Mira's fame and popularity further enraged Rana Vikram. He and his advisors made another attempt on her life. This time they used a viper, of a variety known for its deadly poison. Laid in a jewel box, it was sent to Mira as a present from her brother-in-law, the Rana. She was told that the box contained a precious necklace. The incident is described in one of Mira's poems thus:

---

* Situated near the city of Jaipur in Rajasthan.

Laid in a casket,
   the Rana then sent,
Raging in fury
   a deadly serpent.
"Tell her it is a gift
   of a pearl necklace rare."

This I in ecstasy
   around my neck did wear.
It turned into a string
   of pearls shining and bright;
And lo, my chamber
   was flooded with light.[20]

Like the poison episode, this gift of the snake is mentioned not only by Mira but also by many later poets and devotees in their poems. One can question the veracity of these incidents by suggesting that some good-natured intermediary substituted an innocuous drink for the poison and a real necklace for the snake in order to protect Mira. But this does not diminish Mira's steadfastness, her faith and her deep love for the Lord.

Some scholars maintain that the persecution of Mira was the result of political intrigues. But there is no record to suggest that Mira tried to interfere either directly or indirectly in court affairs at Chittor. She was too deeply engrossed in her love of the Lord to be interested in politics. Saints and devotees have always been persecuted for their bold and unorthodox approach to devotion, their summary rejection of external formalities and their complete disregard for the barriers of caste, colour and creed. It is true that Mira was neither put on the cross nor beheaded, but her lot was in no way easy. Her entire life is a tale of suffering and agony. Slandered by her people, persecuted by her own family and constantly faced with misfortune, she bore everything with an ungrudging fortitude, a saintly tolerance.

Mira never remonstrated with her tormentors, and she could never be provoked to retaliate. She was too kind hearted to utter harsh words, and she had only feelings of sympathy towards her oppressors. She tells the Rana:

> I would have, O Rana,
>   redeemed thy entire fold;
> But they turned a deaf ear
>   to all that Mira told.[21]

An incident recorded in an old narrative throws light on Mira's humility and her spirit of tolerance.[22] A priest, looked upon as a holy man, was staying in Chittor as Mira's guest. One day he got annoyed with Mira for one of her unorthodox songs of devotion. Taking it as a personal insult to his beliefs, he got up from the assembly of devotees, shouting abuses at Mira at the top of his voice. Declaring that he would no more accept Mira's hospitality, he started to walk away. Mira, feeling sorry that someone should be annoyed with her, calmly requested the enraged priest not to abruptly end his sojourn in Chittor, but to stay on according to his original plan. The orthodox priest did not change his mind; but Mira, as was her practice with holy men who came to her, sent gifts of clothes, money and food to him. She had acquired an attitude of mind that was detached and tolerant, and at the same time noble and loving. In one of her poems, using the example of a tree, she says that a devotee should always be large-hearted, tranquil and forbearing:

> Those who come to cut it, it does not hate,
> Nor adores them who come to irrigate.
> Even to those who hurl stones with force
> It yields fruits, with no touch of remorse.

Gales and storms and the fury of rain
It suffers all, yet does not complain.[23]

Mira's devotion, her personality and her songs abounding
with love for the Lord had a powerful impact on those who came
in contact with her. Her palace gates were open for holy men and
they were always well provided with food and clothing. But an
orthodox faction resented her way of devotion and her mounting
influence on the people. Some of them, intent on humiliating her,
persuaded a young brahmin to approach Mira and to tell her that
the Lord had appeared to him and had ordered him to go and
spend a night in the same bed with Mira, and that this was also
the Lord's command for her. Mira, unperturbed at his audacity,
asked him to come in the evening.

Holy men and devotees, at Mira's invitation, gathered in the
courtyard and, as usual, joined Mira in her songs of devotion.
On arrival, the young man was ushered into the palace and welcomed by Mira. He was dismayed to see a couch laid out in the
courtyard with holy men and devotees sitting around it. Picking
up courage, he protested, "But how can I sleep with you in the
presence of so many persons?" Mira calmly replied that her Lord
was ever present and she could not hide anything from Him or
from His devotees, who were a part of her family.

Mira's purity and the sincerity of her reply deeply touched
the young man. Overcome with remorse, he fell at her feet with
tears in his eyes. Mira forgave him and continued to sing the
praises of her Lord. Her face was shining with divine love and the
audience, including the young brahmin, sat spellbound.

The harassment of Mira at the hands of the Rana and his
advisors continued. Holy men and devotees were intimidated and
forced to keep away from her palace. The two attempts on her life
by her own family must have been a painful experience for Mira,
for she finally decided to leave Chittor. Not that she feared for
her life, but her normal devotional activities were hampered and

devotees were persecuted because of her. One night she quietly slipped out of the Fort of Chittor. It must have been a difficult decision for her to make, for a Hindu wife, in those days, would never leave her husband's home despite any torment she had to face. This is probably the reason that Mira patiently endured the taunts of the people and the cruelty of the kings of Chittor for so long.

It is not known when Mira left Chittor, but scholars have deduced that it must have been in 1534, a few months before the storming of Chittor. Had she remained in the fort, she could not have come out unscathed from the catastrophe that befell the inhabitants.

Bahadur Shah, the Sultan of Gujarat, besieged Chittor in 1535 with a large force. Rana Vikram either fled or was helped out of the fort to a place of safety, and Chittor was left without a ruler. But the dowager queens Jawarbai and Karmeti (or Karnavati) took charge of the defence. They gathered loyal and patriotic warriors and defended the fort gallantly. The siege did not last long, for the fort could not be defended against larger numbers and superior arms. Jawarbai died fighting in the battlefield. With her died a large number of housewives who had taken up arms under her leadership. They inflicted heavy losses on the enemy and amazed them with their valour and skill at arms. But Bahadur Shah's forces again gathered and surrounded the fort. Seeing that the defence of Chittor had become impossible, the entire adult and able-bodied male population of Chittor took to arms, attacked the enemy and died fighting, while their wives, under the leadership of Queen Karmeti, committed *jauhar*,* burning

---

* When a fort was unable to be defended, the men would fight to the end while the women prepared a pyre and entered it singing joyful songs of love and valour, preferring death to capture and believing that they would be reunited with their husbands in heaven.

themselves to ashes. Bahadur Shah, though victorious, entered a fort deserted and desolate.

Mira's parents had always sided with the Ranas of Mewar and fought for them. Her father had laid down his life in doing so. But this time Rao Viram Dev, deeply hurt by the Rana's persecution of Mira, did not go to his aid.

Distressed with the treatment she was receiving at Chittor, Mira had left the fort a few months before Bahadur Shah's attack. It is believed that she first went to Merta, her paternal home. She was warmly welcomed by her eldest uncle, Rao Viram Dev, who all along had been a silent spectator of her suffering at Chittor. He was happy to have Mira in Merta once more. But Mira's stay in Merta could not have been a peaceful one. The whole of Rajasthan was dominated by the priestly class, and rituals and superstitions prevailed. Mira's open denunciation of all external formalities, of fasts and pilgrimages, cut at the roots of the age-old traditions:

O friend, the true path to God is that
    of meditation and love.
Adore the Lord; love Him.

If the Lord could be obtained through holy baths,
I would have wished to be a fish.
If by eating berries and wild fruits
    one could attain Him,
Then are not monkeys better placed than we?
If by eating dry leaves one could reach Him,
Should not the goat have done so?...

If worship of stone could lead one to God,
I would have adored a mountain.
But, says Mira, without love, my friend,
You can never meet the Lord.[24]

Such expressions were against all recognized norms of worship. The ridicule and slander that was Mira's lot in Chittor followed her to Merta. Rao Viram Dev loved Mira deeply; his wife had looked after her during her infancy and Mira was the only female child in the family. But the Rao was also a just ruler and an upholder of traditions, both social and royal. He could not put obstacles in the path of his niece, yet he could not displease the elders of his state. The sensitive Mira soon realized his difficulty. One day she quietly left Merta, as she had earlier left Chittor, without any complaint or bitterness.*

Historically, nothing is known about Mira after she left Merta, and traditional accounts differ. It is, however, generally accepted that she visited the town of Vrindavan, supposed to be the place where Lord Krishna spent his childhood days. Mira always sought the company of holy men. In Vrindavan she called on Jiva Gossain, a holy man who was held in great esteem, almost awe, by the people. He worshipped Lord Krishna with the *gopi bhava*, that is, he regarded Lord Krishna as the only man and all other disciples, himself included, as women who adored Lord Krishna. Jiva Gossain also believed in a life of austerity and never looked at the face of a woman.

When Jiva Gossain heard that some devotee named Mira wanted to meet him, he refused to give her an audience, saying he had taken a vow not to see the face of a woman. At this Mira was amused. Though junior to the renowned Gossain, she had sufficient maturity to treat him as an equal. Using the Gossain's own *gopi* doctrine, Mira said that she thought Lord Krishna was the only man in Vrindavan, and she was surprised to find another man there. For the first time someone—and that too a woman—had replied to him with such bold confidence. The veil

---

*Some scholars believe that she had to leave Merta, as the kingdom was lost by Rao Viram Dev in a battle with Rao Maldev of Jodhpur.

of pretension fell from Jiva Gossain's eyes. He came out, bowed to Mira and received her respectfully.

Mira did not stay in Vrindavan for long. The empty ritualism that prevailed in all the holy places in India could not have appealed to her. It is believed that after leaving Vrindavan Mira proceeded towards Gujarat. One of the objects of her trip to Gujarat could have been to meet her Master, Sant Ravidas, who possibly was in Gujarat at that time.* When she reached Dwarka is not known. At the time she left Merta, she was only thirty-six or thirty-eight. Though young, the devotee in her had matured with rich inner experiences and realization, and she had gained a stature of her own.

Mira, it appears, spent quite a few years in Gujarat. She composed numerous poems in the Gujarati language and is looked upon as one of the greatest devotional poets of Gujarati literature. It is presumed that for some time she led a peaceful life there.

Meanwhile, after the fall of Chittor, Rana Vikram, who had run away, was brought back by the nobles to take up once again the reign of the battered kingdom of Mewar. But within a year he was assassinated by Banbir, the illegitimate son of his uncle.† In 1537 Banbir declared himself the Rana. In 1540 Udai Singh, the youngest son of Rana Sanga and Mira's youngest brother-in-law, drove away Banbir with the help of a loyal band of nobles and became the Rana.

Chittor had passed through hard times. Once the seat of a powerful state, it was now reduced to a small principality. An

---

*Ravidas did spend quite some time in Gujarat or kept visiting it. There are, even now, many groups in Gujarat who call themselves the followers of Ravidas. Mira might have spent some time at the feet of her Master until he moved on to some other place.

†Banbir was the illegitimate son of Prince Prithviraj, the elder brother of Rana Sanga.

entire generation of brave men and women had lost their lives in
the wars. People were still suffering from the after-effects of the
catastrophes they had had to face. But Mira was not forgotten.
The poor, low-caste, simple people sang her songs with great
devotion. The public, in general, now started to attribute their
misfortunes to the persecution of Mira. Rana Ratan Singh
had met with a violent death; Rana Vikram, who had tried
to kill Mira, was assassinated; and the people of Chittor, who
had maligned and harassed her, had been ruined. A feeling
of remorse came over them. Mira's life of suffering now drew
public sympathy and people started to adore her. It was felt by
one and all that the Rana, as also the people of Chittor, should
atone for their sins against Mira by bringing her to Chittor and
apologizing to her.

The young Rana Udai Singh, sharing these feelings, sent
a group of brahmins to Dwarka in order to persuade Mira to
return to her home in Chittor.

Mira, however, was a princess no more, nor did she look
upon Chittor as her home. She had broken the chains that had
kept her bound to the house of Mewar. She had no desire to
return to the cage, though a golden one, of the royal palaces.
She was happy with her lot, lost in the love of her beloved Lord.
She refused to return. The insistent pleadings and entreaties of
the brahmins could not persuade her to relent. Exasperated and
afraid of incurring royal displeasure if they returned without
Mira, they decided to give up food until Mira would agree to
accompany them to Chittor.

Mira was in a dilemma. She had no intention of returning
to Chittor; at the same time she could not suffer the idea of the
brahmins dying of starvation at her door. Three or four days
passed. Mira was moved by their plight and in despair, it is said,
she agreed to accompany them the next morning to Chittor. That
evening she entered the temple of Lord Krishna, presumably

for prayer. Next morning when the priests opened the gates of the temple, Mira was not there; only her *odhhanee* (scarf) was found, in the arms of the idol. The priests concluded that Mira had merged into the image of Lord Krishna and had become one with it.

The story immediately caught the imagination of the people. Mira had already become a legend in Rajasthan and such an end lent a touch of glory and even martyrdom to her life. The brahmins, with their problem thus solved, returned to the Rana with the account of the glorious end of a great devotee's life. The kings and nobles of Mewar settled down to their usual court life and Mira was conveniently forgotten, for there is no mention of her in any of the contemporary records of Mewar.

Some modern scholars, however, have taken this incident as evidence of Mira's disappearance, not of her death. Such a disappearance was the only way out of her dilemma. Leaving the temple in the night unnoticed would not have been difficult because the temple—in Mira's time a modest structure—was still in a dilapidated condition after being damaged in 1473 by Sultan Mahmud Begara of Gujarat.* No guards were kept around the temple, and Mira could easily have been helped to escape by a sympathetic devotee.

The date of her disappearance is usually accepted as 1546, when Mira was about forty-eight years old. But in some of her poems she describes herself as having grown old with her hair "turned grey with age". This implies that she lived much beyond the year 1546 and attained an age which could reasonably be termed 'old'.

---

*"The present gigantic Dwarkanathji Temple was erected in the later 18th century by Gopala Naik Tambekar, a Satara banker and statesman. A miniature painting in the Baroda Museum shows the older, very modest shrines built by Maharaja Abhai Singh of Jodpur (1724–1748), and Mira Bai's Temple must have been even smaller." Hermann Goetz, *Mira Bai*, p.28, 31.

Scholars have tried to ascertain the details of Mira's death through the books of the *bhaats** who used to keep records of the royalty of Rajasthan. But their accounts differ.† Kalyansingh Shekhawat, while conducting research on Mira,[25] examined the records of Merta royalty kept by the family priests, wherein it is mentioned that Mira died in 1547 at Dwarka and her body was cremated on the banks of river Gomti, a rivulet running by the side of Dwarka. Dr Shekhawat, on the basis of his inquiries in Gujarat and Rajasthan, and on the basis of the records of the family priests of Merta, concludes that Mira died a natural death in 1547.

At the time of her death Mira was not politically important. The royal families of Merta and Mewar continued to be indifferent to Mira till almost the beginning of the twentieth century.‡ The entries of the *bhaats* and the family priests cannot be treated as reliable, for they must have been made long after Mira's death when they thought her important enough to be mentioned in the records of the royal families. The *bhaats* lived in Rajasthan, and when Mira died they were probably far away from the actual place of her death. What they have recorded is apparently from hearsay, not from direct knowledge. Nevertheless, they point to the fact that Mira had a natural death.

Modern scholars have given different dates for Mira's departure from the world. Agreeing with the dates of the *bhaats*, some

---

* A group of people who kept the records of the main events in the lives of kings and nobles, the descendants of the *bhaats* still preserve the old records.
† According to Bhurdan Bhaat of village Lunve (Rajasthan), Mira died in 1546; he also adds that the place of her death is not known. The *bhaats* of Ranimanga give the date as 1548, while others give it as 1547.
‡ Parashuram Chaturvedi, the well-known scholar of Indian mysticism, writes in a letter to Padmavati Shabnam, "During my trip to Udaipur [the capital city of Mewar, Rajasthan], I came to know that there is little respect or regard for Mira in this town." (*Mira, Vyaktitwa aur Kartritwa*, p.500.)

give it as 1546, 1547, or 1548; while others, on the basis of their own research and deductions, put it between 1563 and 1573.

As already stated, Mira's life story after she left Chittor is based on traditional accounts. Hermann Goetz has tried to trace her life after her disappearance from Dwarka, but he admits that his narration is based "merely on circumstantial evidence, not documentation".[26] According to him, Mira came to North India and spent many years travelling from place to place, spreading her message of devotion. The Ranas of Chittor had already forgotten her and the hidebound traditionalists were relieved at her disappearance. No attempts were made to search for Mira. She could freely move in North India and pursue her spiritual path.

Sant Mat traditions maintain that Mira, after leaving Dwarka, went in search of her Master, Ravidas. But in those days of poor communications, one wonders whether she met him or not. Sant Ravidas himself, like most Saints, was always on the move. Although in 1550, according to some scholars, Ravidas was still living,[*] it seems that Mira could not contact her Master. Some of her songs, addressed to 'Jogi' and believed to be meant for Ravidas, throw light on her longing to meet the Saint and her attempts to find him. In one song she wonders whether her Master has put her out of his mind or he is no more in the world.[†] Suffering deeply in separation and longing to meet her beloved Master, she continued her search for him until she was old.

---

[*] Some scholars maintain that Saint Ravidas lived until 1552.
[†] The poem "Longing for the Jogi" can be found in Part II.

Mira's Message

Mira had no disciples, for she did not initiate anyone. In an often repeated couplet, an unknown medieval poet, paying tribute to Mira, says:

> Listen, O friends of wisdom:
> Mira's name will remain
> Because of her own qualities,
> For she begot no son,
> And she accepted no disciple.

There was no physical or spiritual successor of Mira to preserve her life story or her numerous compositions. Taken purely from oral traditions, her poems were reduced to writing many years after her death. That is the reason they are not available to us in the order in which they were composed. Thus the evolution of the devotee in Mira from the worshipper of the limited to that of the unlimited, the Formless One, though evident from her poems, cannot be traced chronologically. Her praise of idol worship and pilgrimages in some poems and her summary rejection of such external observances in other poems is an apparent contradiction that has led scholars to accept some of her poems as authentic and reject others, according to their own preconceived ideas. But Mira knew her mind, her path and the object of her devotion. The poems available to us are a miscellany of her spiritual experiences at different stages in her spiritual life. They need to be classified according to the state of spiritual development they reflect. But it is an impossible task, for through oral traditions her songs have been mixed together, and the reader is sometimes faced, in the same poem, not only with sudden changes in rhythm and beat, but even in the theme and thought. Mira's poems, as also her life, thus seem destined to remain somewhat of a mystery for all time to come.

Taking into consideration Mira's apparently later songs, or songs reflecting a wider outlook and deeper spiritual experience, it is not difficult to trace similarities between her message and that of other Saints.

Like all Saints, Mira gives great importance to human birth, which she describes as a rare opportunity to attain freedom from the endless cycle of birth and death:

> Rare is the privilege of this human birth;
> This is a chance provided by the Lord
> To ferry across the dreadful ocean.[27]

The soul has been taking birth in this world since the day of creation. Mira, in reply to the Rana, in one of her poems brings out this idea distinctly:

> I have not come to this world
> For the first time, O Rana;
> From the very day of creation
> I have been coming here.

> In this birth I have come to the house of Merta,
> Have been given the name of Mira
> And been married into the Rana family.
> But the soul has neither a family, nor any name.[28]

In the same vein she says in another poem:

> The bangles of eighty-four,*
> Alas, I have worn many a time....
> In different births I had a different spouse.
> But now I have realized that
> My true husband is the eternal Lord.[29]

Even after getting the opportunity of human birth, Mira says that one cannot realize the Lord without the help and guidance of one who knows and has traversed the path leading to Him and who has herself merged into the Lord. In one of her songs she describes God-realization as the soul's wedding. When the soul has been wedded to the Divine Bridegroom, other wedded souls ask her:

> You are blessed, O soul, you are now married,
> But why so long a maid's life did you lead?

To this Mira gives the soul's reply, pointing out that the soul could not be married; that is, the Lord could not be attained earlier, because the soul had not found a Master:

> Until now I met not the Master kind;
> Who else for me, O friend, a match could find?[30]

---

*Refers to the eighty-four hundred thousand (8,400,000) life forms into which the soul keeps reincarnating.

Like all other Saints, Mira stresses the fact that God does not reside in temples and mosques, in holy places or forests. He is within the human body, and only by going within can He be found. She points out that it is only through the Master that one can go within and realize the Lord:

> My Master has revealed to me
> The mirror within my own body;
> Now I'll sing and dance in ecstasy.
>
> Keep to yourself your gems and jewellery;
> I have discarded them all, O Rana.
>
> My true Lord I have come to behold;
> None knows of this wealth within the body.[31]

In another song Mira says that she has become a slave of her beloved Lord. Why need she go to Kashi?* Ganga is within her body, and within is the holy Jamuna;† and within the body resides the everlasting Lord of all.[32]

Describing the body as 'home', Mira conveys her experience of finding the Lord within it:

> O friend, my bliss knows no bounds today,
> For within my home I have discovered
> The beloved Lord.
> For Him I searched in forests,
> Endlessly I sought Him in Vrindaban,
> And all holy places did I scan,
> But could find Him not.

---

* The city of Varanasi, a visit to which is regarded as holy.
† Two rivers in India, a bath in which is regarded as an act of merit.

In the unique casement
On the seventh floor of the mansion within,
I discovered the dear Lord, O friend.[33]

In a song reminiscent of a poem by Guru Amardas[34] that describes the human body as the treasure house of numerous inner worlds, markets, and of the Lord Himself, Mira says:

Realize, O friend, your body,
Like the ocean, is full of treasures.
Open your inner chamber
And light the lamp within.

Within the body are gardens with rare blooms
Where peacocks dance
To the tune of Divine Music.
Within the body is the lake of bliss
In which swans* revel in transports of joy.

In your body is a vast market;
Go within, engage in trade
And reap ever-abiding profit.
Mira sings Thy praises, O Lord,
And begs Thee to give her a lasting abode
At the feet of the Saints.[35]

Mira repeatedly stresses the importance of the practice of Nam, the Name of the Lord. In the terminology of the Saints, Nam is not a written or spoken word. It is the power which has created the entire universe and is sustaining it. The Lord and His Name, according to the Saints, are one and the same. It is the

---

*'Peacocks' and 'swans' refer to souls.

Master who can connect the disciple's soul to the Name which leads to true realization. Mira clearly refers to the supreme power of Nam in her songs:

> O Beloved, I am enamoured of Thy Name.
> Through the practice of Thy Name, I am told,
> Souls, though heavy as stones,
> Can float across with ease to the opposite shore.
> My Master gave me this powerful and mighty Name
> And I recognized my true self.[36]

> I am dyed in the colour of Nam,
> In a hue deep and indelible.
> I drank the cup of this Nectar
> And have ascended within with great force.
> I am intoxicated with the wine of Nam,
> Nothing else appeals to me;
> Worldly pleasures have become insipid.
> Says Mira, O Lord, through Thy Name
> All false colours of the world have dissolved.[37]

It is only the Master who bestows the rare gift of Nam, the "original treasure" of the soul, which cannot be squandered or stolen and which "keeps on increasing from day to day".[38]

This power of Nam manifests within the human body in the form of a divine melody. Saints have variously called it Nam, Shabd, Bani, Dhun. It is the Word of the Bible, Kun or Kalma of the Holy Qur'an and Nad or Akashwani of the Hindu scriptures. Mira refers to Shabd, the sound current or divine melody, in a number of her poems:

> My Master joined me with my source, the Shabd,
> And I'm lost in the power of that sweet Melody.[39]

Ever do I live in the Shabd
My Master blessed me with.[40]

When the soul is tuned to this divine melody by the Master,
the endless chain of transmigration is broken. Mira says that her
Master, by enabling her to hear "the mighty Shabd", has ended
"the torment of birth and death" for her.[41] The Lord can be realized only by merging into Shabd:

> Mira has known the almighty Lord
> By merging in the ocean of Shabd.[42]

The divine melody of Shabd, the sound current, is ever
resounding within the human body. Shabd has the two qualities
of light and sound, which Mira clearly points out:

> Within your body the gong resounds
> In sweet strains of eternal song.
> Within your body of ten doors,
> Day and night rumbles the sound of a drum....
>
> Within your body burns a flame
> In resounding waves of brilliant light.[43]

Utilizing the imagery of tilling the soil, Mira vividly describes
the practice of Nam, the light and sound of Nam, and the place in
the human body where it is contacted. She describes the practice
of Nam as ploughing a field and obtaining a good harvest:

> My farm* yields the crop of the Lord's Name,
> And through Name my soul remains
> absorbed in the Lord.

---

* The human body.

In North India, the area between the two rivers Ganges and Jamuna is regarded as a very fertile agricultural land. Mira refers to the eye centre as that fertile place most suited for raising the crop of Nam. The two rivers are the two paths leading to the left and right from the eye centre. It is between these two paths, that is, at a point behind the two eyes, that the disciple has to concentrate her attention:

> Once I tilled the beds between Ganga and Jamuna,
> And did sow the seed of the Lord's Name.
> It now yields a refulgent crop
> Of diamonds and pearls of rare beauty.

In the human body the seat of the soul, or the 'swan' as Mira calls it in some of her poems, is the eye centre. When the soul, after withdrawing itself from the nine portals of the body, arrives at this point, it sees a brilliant light, described by Mira as the flame:

> The yogis resort to breath control
> And intricate physical ordeals;
> But the eye centre is the seat of the swan,
> Where continually shines a brilliant flame.

Here the soul also comes in contact with Shabd. With the help of surat, the faculty of the soul to hear, and nirat, the faculty of the soul to see, the soul proceeds on its further journey. Continuing the imagery of ploughing the field, Mira says that the faculties of the soul to hear and see are the two bullocks that are pulling the plough. Having attained access to the eye centre, the soul, with the help of surat and nirat, now enjoys the bliss of the sound and light at will:

I have yoked the bullocks of surat and nirat,
And I plough the field
As and when I please.

It is only on reaching the eye centre and coming into contact
with the sound and light of the Shabd that the devotee develops
true love for the Lord:

> Mira's love is now fixed
> At her beloved Lord's feet.[44]

The Master, as already stated, plays an important role in the
soul's journey towards its original home. Through initiation he
imparts the technique of meditation to the disciple and connects
him with Shabd or the sound current within. And when the disciple starts his inner journey, the Master, in his radiant form, guides
and leads him stage by stage to Sat Lok, the abode of the Lord.

Initiation has been described by mystics as a new birth of the
disciple's soul, a birth in the 'house of the Master'. Mira suggests
this thought through the imagery of a traditional Indian daughter's relationship with her father. After birth in the father's house,
the daughter is brought up and educated by him to become a
good wife. The father also arranges the marriage of the daughter
after selecting a suitable groom. In Sant Mat, the Master, like the
father, takes charge of the disciple's soul, helps and guides her
and ultimately becomes instrumental in the soul's union with the
Lord. Mira says that her father is the Master and her husband
resides in Sat Lok:

> Sat Lok is the abode of my spouse,
> And at the feet of the Saints
> Is my true father's home.

She goes on to add:

> Without the beloved Lord,
> I cannot survive;
> Without the Master, at His abode
> I cannot arrive.[45]

Mystics of both the East and West tell us that we all have to experience the results of our karmas or actions, whether the actions be good or bad. "As we sow, so shall we reap" is the law. The soul has to take birth again and again to gather the fruit of its actions, good actions being as binding as bad ones. This law of cause and effect, known as the law of karma, is inviolable. Mira refers to the karma theory in some of her poems. In reply to the Rana's directive that she should abide by the protocol and traditions of the royal family, Mira says:

> All relationships in this world
> Are the result of past karmas;
> Family bonds are meaningless.
> It is seen in the world
> That two sons of the same mother
> Have different roles to play in life
>   (according to their karmas);
> One sits on the throne while the other
> Subsists through ploughing the fields....
>
> All associations in this world
> Are the result of our karmas
>   and are not lasting.[46]

In another small poem Mira further explains the karma theory:

Life in the world is but brief and fleeting;
Why should you involve yourself in it?
Father and mother gave you birth,
But the Creator gave you karmas,
According to which you have got the body.

Whatever you enjoy, whatever you spend,
Whatever deeds of charity you perform,
Their results you will experience.
The account of your actions, of what you
Have given and what you have taken,
Alone will go with you after death.
Nothing else will accompany you.

Mira says, this is your chance
    to worship the Lord
And ferry across the dreadful ocean
Of birth and rebirth.[47]

Mind and maya are two intractable obstacles on the path of God-realization. Mind is deeply attached to the objects and pleasures of the world and keeps running after them. It is never still, always thinking of something, ever brooding on worldly forms and faces. Mira describes the mind's habit of wandering as its "mercurial ways",[48] which it gives up only when it experiences a joy higher and more lasting than the ephemeral pleasures of the world. That lofty joy is derived from contact with the divine melody of Shabd. Mira says that her mind, which for ages was completely oblivious of the spiritual bliss within, became aware of it on listening to the Shabd of the Master:

My mind, birth after birth lost in slumber,
Awoke on hearing the Shabd my Master gave.[49]

Mira compares the stubborn and wayward habits of the mind with those of a rogue elephant, which can only be tamed by the goad wielded by an expert trainer:

> My mind is like a rogue elephant,
> Wilful, wicked and wild;
> Place thy hand on my head like a goad,
> O Master, and tame this wayward mind.[50]

By its long and incessant indulgence in sense pleasures, by its deep and unremitting attachment to the world and its objects, the mind has accumulated thick layers of dross. Mira says that the Master is an adept washerman who can cleanse our mind of all its impurities. With simran or constant remembrance of the Lord as the 'soap' and love as the 'water', the Master washes the disciple's mind, which once thus washed will never again be covered by dross:

> If Master, the washerman, washes your mind,
> It will never be soiled again....
>
> With remembrance as the soap,
> And love as the water,
> Your mind, cleansed of all blemish,
> With virtue will shine.
>
> So deftly will the washerman scrub it clean,
> Even a speck of dirt it shall not gather again.[51]

Maya or the illusory lure of the world, along with worldly cravings and desires, are the other obstacles on the path. Employing her favourite imagery of a newly wed Indian bride, Mira hints at the obstacles of maya and desires on the way to union with the Lord. The bride wants to go and meet her beloved husband, but according to the custom in Mira's times, she has to go to his chamber all alone and unnoticed by anyone. Her path, however, is obstructed by her mother-in-law (Maya), who is sleeping on the terrace, and by her sister-in-law (worldly desires), who is in the courtyard. The way to her husband's chamber is through the courtyard (the human body) and the terrace (the eye centre):

> Mother-in-law is sleeping on the terrace,
> And sister-in-law in the courtyard.
> My Beloved rests within the chambers above.
> How am I to go and awaken Him?

And Mira adds:

> O thou darling of the Lord,
> Thou must awaken thy Beloved;
> Be alert, O friend, reach Him
> And be in His resplendence.

Concluding the poem, Mira says:

> Awake, O friend, lost in delusion.
> Mira went and met her Beloved
> And became free from the grip of illusion. [52]

Mystics have extolled the benefits of satsang, the association with truly evolved souls, that is, the Saints. The wayward mind is subdued through the company of the Saints and in the course of time acquires the colour of divine love. In a Gujarati poem, Mira says:

Today I have been blessed
By the company of the Saints;
It is a matter of great good fortune for me.

Always remain in the company of Saints.
Through their association you will be dyed
In a divine hue of manifold splendour.
Keep not the company of the evil,[*]
For it will prove a hindrance to your meditation.

The merit of all pilgrimage is at the Saints' feet;
Their feet are holier than the holy waters
Of a million Gangas and Jamunas....

Mira declares that she has learnt
Of the qualities of the Lord
Through the company of Saints.
She will always remain in their company
And ever bask in the sunshine
Of the dust of their lotus feet.[†53]

In another lyric Mira urges people to seek the company
of Saints:

Taste the nectar of satsang, O friends,
O taste thou the elixir of satsang....

---

[*] Mira uses the word *saakat* here, a word used for evil persons who are completely under the domination of the mind.
[†] The lotus flower is associated with purity, delicacy, beauty; although it grows in mud and water, it remains untouched by them. Out of reverence, the feet of a holy man or deity are referred to as lotus feet. The term 'lotus feet' particularly refers to the feet of the Radiant Form of the Master.

In minutes satsang will lead to salvation;
Thus avow the Vedas and all holy books.[54]

Herself dyed in the sublime hue of satsang, Mira sings in ecstasy:

The Saints alone are my dear ones;
I belong to them, my very life are they.
Mira remains merged in the Saints' company,
As butter abides within milk.[55]

The inner spiritual experiences of all mystics, whether of the East or the West, are the same. Like Namdev, Kabir, Paltu and other Saints, Mira gives indications of her inner experiences in some of her poems:

O friend, the firmament within
Resounds with the divine melody.
Listen, my soul, to the clanging sound
That reverberates without any cymbals.
On the peak of Sunn* burns a lamp;
Forever it burns without any wick or oil.[56]

Describing the bliss of one of the inner regions Mira says:

In Bhanwar Gupha† revel bumblebees‡
    in joy around flowers of bliss,
Flowers whose fragrance overwhelms
    them with ecstasy.

---

* The third stage in the soul's journey in the inner spiritual regions.
† The fourth stage in the soul's journey within.
‡ Souls.

Within Bhanwar Gupha swing souls in exuberance;
Souls, who on getting the body
    of five elements,*
Did light the lamp of divine knowledge within it.

My eyes, oblivious of all else now, gaze
    at the Beloved without blinking.
The stupor caused by endless wanderings
    has vanished,
And the Beloved speaks to Mira directly.[57]

Love and longing are the underlying currents that run through Mira's poems. Her own life is one long tale of pain and suffering in the separation from her beloved Master and the Lord. According to Mira, love came to her as a gift from her Master, and so did longing:

My Master has shot me
    with perfect aim,
With an arrow tempered
    in longing's flame.[58]

Love is the precursor; longing follows in its wake. It is longing, the pain of separation, that develops and strengthens love. Mira says that it was through her yearning for the Beloved that her love grew and engulfed her entire being. In a well-known lyric she says:

Watering with my surging tears,
I have nurtured love's tender vine;

---

* The human body, which consists of the five elements: earth, water, fire, air and ether.

Now it has spread and matured,
And the rare fruit of bliss it bears.[59]

Mira's hymns of union with the Lord are full of exuberance. Their warmth and verve is made all the more captivating by the tenderness of her devotion. In the following poem, she conveys her feelings of joy and bliss through an allusion to the change brought about by the onset of the monsoon in a land scorched by drought:

It's raining today, let it pour;
My love is home, Him I adore.

Dense clouds in the sky now hover;
In tender drops do they shower.
Lakes and ponds that were dry and drained
Becoming full have their joy regained....

For Him many days did I pine;
I've met Him, and now He is mine....

It's raining today, let it pour;
My love is home, Him I adore.[60]

In another song of unaffected beauty, Mira says:

My dear Lord brought me to His heart;
Not for a moment will I let Him part.
Fondly to Him now I will cling;
His praises with joy will I sing.

To my Beloved's charming eyes,
My entire being I sacrifice.

Them do I love, them I adore,
Again and again, evermore.[61]

The eloquence of love and the poignancy of her yearning have
made Mira's poems deeply moving. Her expressions of the joy of
union or the pain of separation are neither a poetic fancy nor an
attempt at lyrical adornment; they are the unaffected and spontaneous revelations of her own experience. The profundity of her
expressions, as also their amazing simplicity, are both penetrating
and inspiring. For these qualities Mira stands foremost among the
devotional poets of her times. Her lyrics of longing have been very
popular with devotees, as also with the masses, for their depth
of feeling, for their delicacy of expression and for the intensity of
their effect. These qualities run through most of her poems:

His image, after luring my heart,
Keeps rankling like a pointed dart.
Without seeing Him, I will for sure
Lose my life. Only the healing herb
Of His look can my suffering cure....

Her very self to the Lord has Mira sold,
To ever remain in His loving fold.
Since the day my Lord His darshan gave,
For a glimpse of Him my eyes still crave.[62]

The magnitude of her anguish is brought out by Mira in
another poem, in a simple but effective manner:

On the gallows is laid my bed;
How can I get a moment's sleep?
In the sky within is spread
The couch of my Beloved;

Access to Him how can I gain?
O friend, in love I am insane;
None knows my suffering, nor my pain.

The wounded alone will know
The anguish of the wounded,
Or He who has dealt the blow....

Like a wounded beast, vale to vale
I run in pain; I cannot endure.
No healer could I ever find
Who my constant agony could cure.
Then alone will I be rid of misery
When my Lord comes as the healer to me.[63]

So great is Mira's suffering in separation from the Loved
One that she announces that had she known of the torment one
has to undergo on the path of love, she would have warned all of
this danger:

I would have called to the beat of drum:
None, oh none, in love's lane should come.[64]

Despite all the pangs of separation, despite all her tears and
sighs, Mira is not prepared to give up the path of love. She longs
for her Master's darshan, a glimpse of his beautiful face; she ear-
nestly prays for it, but there is no insistence on her part that he
should give in to her appeal. For the true lover is only concerned
with what pleases the beloved, concerned only with the will of
the beloved. She completely surrenders herself to the will of the
loved one. In her poems, Mira repeatedly prays to the Lord to
grant her the refuge of her Master's feet. In her prayers to the
Master, she entreats him to redeem her from this world of pain

and turmoil, only if he deems fit. In a poem, replying to some of
her critics, she says:

> I have met my Master Raidas, who has given me
>   the secret of true knowledge....
> I will live in the will of my Master,
>   who is supreme for me,
> And abandoning my ego,
>   take refuge at his lotus feet.[65]

A well-known poem of Mira, addressed to her Master,
illustrates the sensitive, yet ardent nature of her love. Addressing
him as 'Jogi' she says:

> Do not go, O Jogi, pray do not go.

But if the Master has to leave her, then Mira requests:

> The path of love is unfamiliar and intricate;
> Pray, put me on the lane [that leads to thee].

If it is not possible for him to do so, then Mira has another
boon to ask from him:

> Let me prepare a funeral pyre built with sandalwood
>   and adorned with aromatic herbs;
> With thine own hands set fire to it.

For she feels that she would not be able to remain alive if the
Master left her. The longing to be always in the physical presence
of the Master is next expressed by Mira:

> And when I am burnt and reduced to ashes,
>   pray smear thy body with them.

True love is losing one's identity into that of the Beloved, becoming one with Him. To become one with the Lord is the goal of all divine love. Mira, concluding the poem, brings out this longing to become one with the object of her love:

> Before leaving, pray, merge my flame
> into thy flame, O Master.[66]

Mira, like most North Indian Saints, has used words and idioms of different languages and dialects in her compositions. Besides Hindi and Gujarati, she has freely borrowed words and expressions from Braj, Avadhi, Marwari (and its dialects), Bhojpuri, Maithili, Sanskrit, Arabic, Persian and even Punjabi. In Bengal her poems are very popular; in Maharashtra, poet-saints like Tukaram have referred to her with great regard; and Mahipati, the poet-biographer of the Saints of Maharashtra, has been eloquent in his praise of Mira.

All over India, Mira's poetry is appreciated for its simplicity and unadorned fervour, its spontaneity of expression and the loftiness of her theme rendered in simple yet elegant words. She is loved for the lyrical quality of her verse unalloyed with artifice, for her chaste and graceful use of similes, and for the ease and fluency of her expression. In the deeply emotional content of her poetry, her exuberance in the depiction of her love, and above all the tender yet poignant revelation of her anguish in separation from the Beloved, Mira, perhaps, has few equals.

PART II

Selected Poems

Ferry Me Across

The fetters of a person's own past karmas or actions keep him bound to the physical world. They are the cause of the unending round of birth and death through which he keeps going. There is no true happiness in this world of sorrow and pain. Mira prays to the Lord to ferry her across this ocean of turmoil.

> The entire world is tossing
> Endlessly in the vortex
> Of the terrible eighty-four.*
> Mira implores Thee, dear Lord,
> Rescue her from the whirl
> Of birth and death.
>
> Born in this vale of tears,
> I have suffered great misery.
> Pray, dispel the sombre clouds
> Of worldly sorrow and pain.
> The fetters of my own karmas
> Bind and torment me.
> Shatter them, beloved Lord.
>
> Ferry me across, O Lord.
> At Thy lotus feet I bow
> Again and again, and pray:
> Dear Lord, ferry me across.

> *Mira Sudha Sindhu,*[†] p.351
> *Hari mane paar utaar*

---

* The 8,400,000 life forms into which the soul keeps reincarnating.
† Hereafter referred to as *MSS*.

Love's Complaint

In this small poem Mira longs for the Lord who, after giving her the blessing of His love, has left her forlorn to suffer the pangs of separation.

> Where have you gone, dear Lord,
> After planting your love in my heart?
> You have forsaken me, O deceitful one,
> After setting the wick of love aflame.
> After launching love's boat, you have
> Left it adrift in the sea of separation.
> Beloved Lord, when will you meet me?
> Mira can live no more without you.

MSS, p.164
Prabhuji then kahaan gaya

A Petition

Mira, in this poem, appeals to the Lord to deliver her from the sufferings of the world. However, in complete surrender to Him she asks the Lord to do so only if such is His will.

My merciful Lord,
Pray hear my petition –
I am drifting in the world's stormy sea;
Rescue me, if it be Thy will.

No one in this world is mine,
Thou alone art truly my own.
Father, mother, son, kinfolk:
All are companions for their own ends.
Listen to Mira's prayer, O Beloved –
If it be Thy will, unite her to Thy feet.

MSS, p.325
Tum sunau dayaal mhaanri arji

Mira's Agony

Mira prays to the Lord to come and grant His vision to her. Day and night she is restless without seeing Him. She has lost all desire for food and in her yearning is unable to sleep. She finds no words to tell the tale of her suffering and invokes the All-knowing One to come and meet her.

Come, beloved Lord,
Grant me Thy darshan;
Away from Thee
I cannot stay alive.

Like the lotus without water,
Like the night without moon,
Is Thy dear one
Without Thee, O Lord.

In anguish I wander day and night,
And pangs of separation
Keep gnawing at my heart;
Days drag without hunger,
Nights without sleep,
And lips fail to narrate
The tale of my grief.

What can I say? I have no words
To convey my longing;
Pray, come and quench
This fire that's searing my heart.
Lord, you know all;
Then why do you torment me thus?
Pray, have mercy;
Come and meet Mira
Who, forever your slave,
In love surrenders at your feet.

Mira Brihat Padavali, p.133
Pyaare darshan deejo aay

---

* Hereafter referred to as *MBP.*

All Roads Closed

Mira, yearning to be back with the Lord, complains of the oppressive design that He has contrived. He has made her residence in a land far away from her true home of love and bliss. All the paths of return seem to be blocked. The way back, beset with pitfalls and dangers, is hard to tread. Worldly desires and temptations are the sentinels that stop her at every step; the five passions are the robbers that deprive her of all merit. She concludes the song on a happy note, saying that her Master has revealed the Lord to her and brought her back home.

> The four lanes are blocked;*
> How am I to go and meet the Lord?
>
> Tortuous and slippery is the path;
> My feet find no hold.
> With caution and deliberation
> I take each step,
> But again and again I stumble and fall.
> Steep is the climb to my Beloved's palace;
> I am unable to ascend and reach it.
> The four lanes are blocked;
> How am I to go and meet the Lord?

---

* The four lanes, according to some scholars, refer to the four paths of *gyan* (intellect), *yoga* (breath control and other exercises), *karma* (action) and *vairag* (renunciation).

Far is the dwelling of my Beloved;
The path is narrow, hard to tread,
And my soul quivers at every step.
At every bend stand sentinels to stop me;*
At each step robbers in ambush lie.†

Lord, what an oppressive design
Have you wrought!
In a distant land
You have made my dwelling,
And all the roads are blocked;
How am I to reach you, O Lord?

The true Master has revealed
Mira's Lord to her.
Mira, separated for eons,
He has brought back home.

MSS, p.171
Gali to chaaron band hui

---

* Worldly desires and attractions.
† The five passions of lust, anger, attachment, avarice and ego.

Flame Merging into Flame

This song is a prayer to the Lord from an anguished heart longing for union with Him. Mira tells us that her longing was fulfilled when she met her Master, Sant Ravidas, who put her on the path and enabled her to become one with the Supreme Being.

O Lord of the forlorn, open your eyes;
For long have I stood
Awaiting your one loving look.

Friends and family have turned into enemies;
They shun me like poison.
Except you, in this world,
Dear Lord, I have no friend;
My boat is tossing in the sea.

Restlessly I pass my days;
Without sleep I pass my nights.
I wither as I stand and stand
Awaiting you, dear Lord.

Like an arrow the pangs of separation
Rankle within my heart;
Never for a moment can I forget you.

Ahilya lay in the woods, turned to stone;[*]
Gladly you ferried her across.
What is Mira's weight compared to hers –
A mere pound to a ton!

When Raidas, the true Master, I met,
The severed twig joined again the tree.
My Master revealed the secret of the Name;
The flame of Mira merged into the Flame.

Mirabai ki Shabdavali, p.31
Tum palak ughaarro deenaanaath

---

[*] The wife of Gautama, a Rishi in Hindu mythology. By a curse she was turned into a large stone and for centuries lay in a forest. When Lord Ram passed that way, she was liberated by the touch of his feet.

Sleepless Nights

This poem describes the state of longing and pain in the devotee's heart. Mira says that only one who has undergone this pain can know the intense agony of her separation from the Lord.

I don't have a wink of sleep;
The night seems to be endless.
Will ever my misery end?
Will ever dawn alight?

In dreams if I lose Him,
With a start I wake up.
Even the cool moonbeam
Is searing my heart.

I languish in agony,
And my death is nigh.
O my merciful Lord,
Will I ever meet Thee?

I'm oblivious of my body;
I've grown frantic with pain.
Can others ever know
The torment I suffer?

He alone knows the ache
Who has suffered the pangs;
Mira's life and death now,
O Lord, are in Thy hands.

MSS, p.164
Neendarrli nahin aavai

Repeat the Lord's Name

Mira urges everyone to repeat the Lord's Name. The Name puri-
fies the mind and destroys the vast store of karmas which are
the cause of the soul's repeated incarnation into this world. The
nectar of the Name is offered to humankind by the Saints free of
cost. Why should one hesitate to take it, asks Mira.

My mind now repeats
Only the Lord's Name.

Repeat the Lord's Name, O friend;
It washes off a million sins.
The records of your actions
Of numerous previous births
In no time are torn to tatters
On repetition of the Name.

When nectar in a cup of gold
Is offered to you free,
Why should you be loath to drink it?
Says Mira, let the eternal Lord
Now permeate your body and heart.

MBP, p.218
Mero man raamhi raam rattai re

The Five-Coloured Garment

A small girl, when given new clothes to wear, runs to show them off to her playmates, who are usually playing in an alcove of shrubs. Their favourite game is hide-and-seek. She joins them at play, but when it is her turn to catch an opponent she finds the scarf of her dress, used for covering the head, an obstacle in running. She drops it and runs to find the playmate who is hiding.

Mira uses this imagery to illustrate the soul's journey within. The soul, adorned with the new garment dyed in the colour of the five Melodies, goes to play in the arbour within. She divests herself of the scarf of external observances, which is an encumbrance in her way, and succeeds in finding her Master. Mira gives hints of her inner experience in this poem. She points out that the five elements (earth, water, fire, air and ether), as also the regions of the sun, the moon and the stars, will be left behind, and the soul will soar into still higher regions. She also points out that the Lord is within the body and is revealed in the light emanating from the lamp of love.

> I am infused in the Lord's hue, O friend.
> Pray, get my garment dyed in five colours*
> So I may go and play in the arbour.
> Within the alcove† I will meet my Master;
> Shedding all falsity, I'll sing in joy.‡

---

* The reference here is to the five melodies of the Word or sound current.
† The narrow path beyond the eye centre.
‡ Continuing the imagery, Mira says that she will divest herself of the dress of false beliefs, which are a hindrance in going within and meeting the Master in his radiant form.

The sun will perish, so too the moon;
Earth and sky will exist no more.
Air and water will also go;
The Eternal alone will there be.

Of surat and nirat make the lamp,*
And let thy longing be the wick.
In this lamp pour the oil from love's mart;
Day and night it will keep burning bright.

They write letters whose spouses are afar.
My Beloved resides in my heart;
I need go nowhere to search for Him.

I live not with my parents,
Nor with my in-laws.
Ever do I live in the Word
My Master blessed me with.

Not mine nor thine is this house,† O friend;
Mira lives absorbed in the Lord's hue.

Mirabai ki Shabdavali, p.8
Sakhi ri main to girdhar ke rang raati

---

*Surat and nirat: the faculties of the soul to hear and to see.
† The human body, being perishable, should not be treated as ours; may also
refer to the world, which is not our lasting abode.

The Rare Toy

When a child is given an attractive toy, he becomes fully engrossed in it. Using this image, Mira says that she has obtained
the precious toy of the Lord's Name. She found it in the temple
of her body, and it came with a melodious sound. It is a rare
and priceless thing. Rishis and munis, seers and ascetics could
not get it in spite of all their austerities, penances and strenuous
practices. It is only to be found beyond the region of matter, mind
and maya (illusion). The abode of this Name is in the ineffable
regions of pure spirit. Mira has become one with what others
describe as invisible and unattainable.

> I have obtained the rare toy of His Name;
> O Rana, a precious toy have I found.
>
> Chiming sweetly it entered my temple;[*]
> No hands ever gave it a form or shape.
>
> Great seers and ascetics toiled and toiled,
> But never on this toy could they lay their hands.
>
> It is beyond the plain and peak of Sunn;
> 'Imperceptible' and 'Inaccessible'
> Are the names they have given it.
>
> To her almighty Lord Mira does cling;
> In Him she rests as the gem in a ring.

MSS, p.270
Raam ramkanddu jaddiyun re raanaaji

---

[*] The human body has been described as the temple of God by mystics of the
East and West.

The Day Is Short

After a long period of darkness the light of human birth has come. People must make the most of this opportunity and try to move swiftly on the path to God-realization. Giving up all other cares, they should worry only about reaching their true home before the day of human life fades into the shadows of death. Mira concludes the poem by saying that the Lord has blessed her with a path that is both easy and short.

> Foolish wayfarer, why do you delay?
> Take heed, the day is short,
> And long is your way.
>
> The sun in the east has lit the torch;
> Now is the time for your homeward march.
> Move swiftly, reach home
> Before the sun turns pale;
> The hours are fleeting and long is your trail.
> Treasure the chance, don't falter or lose heart;
> Be free of all cares and make a start.
>
> Reach home, and from fear and doubt be free;
> Loitering midway, you will come to misery.
> Foolish wayfarer, why do you delay?
> Long is the way and soon will end the day.
>
> O kind Lord of Mira, Thou in Thy grace
> Gave her a path, short and easy to pace.

MSS, p.762
Ab kyon kare re moorakh

Mira in Torment

In this poem, Mira tells us of her suffering in the absence of her Beloved. Her long separation from Him has caused her pain and anguish so deep as to make her accuse her Beloved of having acquired the habit of tormenting her.

> Will someone bring me the news
> That my Lord is coming?
> Yes, news of His coming
> That my heart ever longs for.
>
> He comes not Himself;
> He does not send even a letter.
> It has become His habit
> Thus to torment me.
>
> These two eyes of mine
> Listen not to my pleas;
> They flow like a river
> In the monsoon.
>
> I am utterly helpless;
> I know not what to do.
> If I had a pair of wings,
> I would have flown to you.
>
> Mira asks, O Lord,
> When will you meet her?
> She has lost her heart
> To your subtle ways.

MBP, p.53
Koi kahiyau re prabhu aavan ki

Longing for the Jogi

Mira has composed many songs addressed to the 'Jogi'. Most of them are full of love and longing for the one whom she calls the Jogi. Scholars have interpreted them as songs addressed to the Lord, whom she has, in her love, named 'the Jogi'.

In Rajasthan 'jogi' used to be a term applied to almost all types of holy men. To this day, in some parts of Rajasthan, holy men are called jogis. In this, as also in the next two lyrics, it becomes evident that Mira is longing for a glimpse of a person whom she has met in the physical body. In the first poem, she expresses the feeling that either the Jogi has forgotten her or he is no more in the world. In the next one, she says that she has not seen another face as beautiful and radiant as that of the Jogi and she longs to see that face again. In the third poem, she conveys her anguish at not being able to find him in spite of all her efforts to do so, and she has now become feeble and old.

It may not be wrong to conclude that these songs are the expression of Mira's deep love and longing for her Master, Sant Ravidas, whom she has addressed as the Jogi.

> Beloved Jogi, day and night,
> Longingly do I await you.
> The path to you is arduous,
> Narrow and hard; my feet find no hold.
>
> When you did come to my town,
> You found me lacking in my love.
> In my ignorance I erred
> And did not prevail upon you to stay.
>
> For days and days have I waited,
> But, O Jogi, you have not come.

Pray, give your darshan now,
And quench the raging fire of separation,
Which is scorching my entire being.

Either my beloved Jogi
Is no more alive in this world,
Or else he has forgotten me.
What am I to do, O friend,
Where can I go for solace?
Shedding tears in longing
My eyes have come to lose their sight.

O Jogi, I'm in torment within;
Remember that I am your own
And come, end my suffering.
Mira languishes in agony;
Without you she writhes
Like a fish out of water.

MBP, p.80
Jogiaaji nis-din jo'oon baat

Love for the Jogi leads to sorrow.
There's no pleasure in his love,
For the Jogi is no one's friend.

Without thee, O Jogi, I'm restless;
Day and night I pine for thee.

In this entire world,
Nowhere have I seen
A face as radiant
And beautiful as thine.

Thou art Mira's beloved lord.
Pray, when wouldst thou meet her?
Only on meeting thee
Will Mira be happy.

MBP, p.84
Jogia son preet kiyaan dukh hoy

O Jogi! Only thy darshan will
Ease my suffering and anguish;
Else for me life in this world
Is one of unending misery.
Day and night, each moment do I
Pine and languish without thee.

Insane in my longing for a sight of thy face,
I have wandered searching for thee
In all directions, to no avail.
Mira, thy slave, has grown feeble,
And her once dark tresses
Have turned grey with age.

MSS, p.928
Jogi mhaane daras diyaan

Firm Resolve

Mira is resolved to remain in the company of Saints. Wealth, reputation and the comforts of the world she has renounced in order to obtain the blessing of divine love. She is even ready to lay down her life. Her mind is absorbed in simran* and she longs only for rest at her Master's feet.

> Let people try to restrain me,
> O friend; I will not be stopped.
> I will remain in the Saints' company
> And gain the bliss of the Lord's love.
>
> I will not be bothered with the world.
> If all my wealth goes, let it go;
> Even if my head be severed,
> I will not complain.
>
> My mind is absorbed in simran;
> I meet all censure with cheer.
> Mira's Lord, Thou Everlasting One,
> Grant me the shelter
> Of my Master's feet.

MSS, p.391
Barji main kaahooki naahin rahoon

---

*Repetition through a prescribed technique of certain names given by a Master.

The Beloved Comes Home

Mira has composed a number of poems giving expression to her joy at her union with the Lord. Most of them are as full of emotion as her better-known poems of longing. Here Mira sings of the bliss she feels at the arrival of her Beloved and the end of her misery in separation and duality.

The one I longed for has come home;
The raging fire of separation is quenched.
Now I rejoice with Him, I sing in bliss.

The peacocks at the cloud's roar
Dance with unbound joy;
I rejoice in ecstasy
At the sight of my Beloved.

I am absorbed in His love;
My misery of wandering
In the world has ended.
The lily bursts into bloom
At the sight of the full moon;
Seeing Him, my heart blossoms in joy.
Peace permeates this body of mine;
His arrival has filled my home with bliss.

That very Lord has become my own
Who is ever the redeemer of His devotees.
Mira's heart, scorched by the blaze of separation,
Has become cool and refreshed;
The pain of duality has vanished.

MSS, p.510
Mhaara olagia ghar aaya ji

Be Steadfast

Mira calls upon the devotee to be steadfast in his devotion and persist in his spiritual practice. Through the example of a warrior who, equipped with a shield, armour and weapons, valiantly wages war with a determination to win, Mira points out the qualities that the disciple should inculcate within himself. His strength is his Master, his shield is the Master's hand of protection and his sword is the Master's grace. With faith in the Master he should continue his meditation until the object is attained.

Engage in the Lord's devotion;
Persist in your meditation –
Be steadfast.

Far is the abode of the Lord,
Like the fruit of the date-palm tree.
He who climbs and reaches the top
Tastes the sweet fruit of love;
They come to ruin
Who slip and fall.

Why don the armour?
Why seek the safety of a shield?
He is the true warrior who,
Unarmed, charges with all his might;
For the Master is his armour and his shield.

With the dagger of knowledge,
With the Master's grace as the scimitar
And with the lance of detachment,
Take to the field – wage the war;
Never will you face defeat.

Remember, your body is but fragile –
Composed of flesh, bones and nerves
And endowed with ten senses.*
Mira's Lord alone is everlasting;
To Him she is firmly tied
By the delicate twine of love.

MSS, p.750
Lag rahna, lag rahna hari bhajan men

---

* The ten senses: five of action and five of perception.

Why Art Thou Piqued?

This poem of Mira is full of love and longing for the Lord. In the pain of separation she feels that the Lord is annoyed with her. With loving humility she asks Him which out of her numerous faults has offended Him.

Thou art piqued, dear Lord,
Pray, for which fault of mine?
Tell me, of my countless faults,
Which hast Thou taken to heart,
Thus constantly to torment me
In Thy separation's agony?

I am from life to life
Thy ever-sinning slave;
A boundless ocean of virtue
Art Thou, my beloved Lord.

For which failing of mine
Hast Thou taken offence?
Does not Thy heart also,
In mercy, ache at my suffering?

I beseech Thee, overlook my failings
And bless me with Thy darshan,
For ages seem to have passed
Without a glimpse of Thee.

Mira's Lord, Thou Everlasting One,
I repeat Thy Name, I long for Thee.

MBP, p.60
Girdhar roosanoon ji kon gunhaan

Sold to the Saints

This poem is Mira's reply to her sister-in-law Udabai, who at the bidding of the Rana* comes to plead with her to give up the company of the Saints.

> Mira's state is no secret to the world;
> Try to understand, my good Udabai.
>
> The Saint alone is my father and mother;
> He is my family, friend and guide.
> I live in surrender at the lotus feet
> Of my Master, day and night.
>
> Go back and enlighten the Rana;
> I will listen not to your sermons.
> Almighty is Mira's Lord;
> She has sold herself to the Saints.

MSS, p.268
Meeraan baat naheen jag chhaani

---

* The kings of Mewar were known as Ranas. The Rana referred to in this poem was the brother of Mira's husband.

Mira Is Steadfast

This is another poem with an autobiographical touch, describing how Mira stood up boldly against all the torments inflicted upon her by her brother-in-law, the ruler of Mewar. Here she expresses her firm resolve to follow the path of devotion. Her Master has shown her the mirror within the body, her soul is shining bright and she is lost in the Lord's love.

> I will not be restrained now, O Rana,
> Despite all you do to block my path.
>
> I have torn off the veil of worldly shame;
> Only the company of Saints is dear to me.
>
> Merta, my parents' home, I have left for good.
> My surat and nirat, awakened,
> Now shine bright.
>
> My Master has revealed to me
> The mirror within my own body;*
> Now I'll sing and dance in ecstasy.
>
> Keep to yourself your gems and jewellery;
> I have discarded them all, O Rana.
>
> My true Lord I have come to behold;
> None knows of this wealth within the body.

---

*Just as a mirror reflects a person's image, Mira implies that by going within through the help of her Master, she has realized her true self.

I fancy not your forts and palaces
Nor want silken robes wrought with gold.

Mira, unadorned and unbedecked,
Roams intoxicated in the Lord's love.*

MSS, p.280
Raana ji ab na rahoongi tori hatki

---

* In some versions of this poem, there is an additional line: I met Raidas, my
Master, perfect and kind; through him I obtained the elixir of knowledge.

Love's Reproach

Mira, in a piquant mood, accuses the Lord of heartlessness, for after giving her the joy of divine love, He now makes her drink from the bitter cup of separation. The apparent harsh tone of accusation acquires a lyrical softness through the underlying tender feelings of Mira's love.

My winsome Lord, you have no heart;
I've seen your love, I know your art.

When first I fell in your love's snare,
Lost in love, I wasn't aware
That one so loving, tender and kind
Would swiftly cast me off His mind.
My winsome Lord, you have no heart;
I've seen your love, I know your art.

First you offered love's nectar sweet;
Now you give me poison to eat!
Tell me, Lord, come tell me, pray,
Where did you learn this callous way?
My winsome Lord, you have no heart;
I've seen your love, I know your art.

Eternal Lord, to you Mira bends;
You love only for selfish ends.
My winsome Lord, you have no heart;
I've seen your love, I know your art.

MSS, p.178
Jaao hari nirmohia

I Will Not Blink

Mira tells us that once she is face to face with the Lord, she will not let Him be out of sight even for an instant. She also gives hints of her inner spiritual progress.

> Looking at Him will my eyes remain occupied,
> O friend, when I meet the dear Lord.
> He'll ever dwell within my eyes;
> I'll blink not, lest He go out of sight.
>
> From the window high in Trikuti's* palace
> I'll peer, and look for Him, O friend.
> I'll fix my attention in the chamber of Sunn,[†]
> And there place my couch[‡] in blissful ecstasy.
>
> O Mira's Beloved, Thou Almighty One,
> I'll render myself in oblation to Thee.[§]

MBP, p.127
Nainan banaj basaaoon ri

---

* Trikuti is the second stage in the spiritual journey of the soul within. It is the region of Brahm or the universal mind. Mira suggests that it is only after reaching Trikuti that the soul can look forward to going further and meeting the Lord.
[†] The third stage in the soul's journey within.
[‡] Await Him.
[§] 'Oblation' and 'sacrifice', two words commonly used by Indian mystics, are not to be confused with any sacrificial ritual. To convey the idea of complete surrender of body, mind and soul to the Master or the Lord, and of loving submission to His will, the mystics have used certain terms which, in the absence of any other suitable word, have been translated as 'oblation' and 'sacrifice' in this as also in some other poems.

The Lord's Slave

Mira, in this short poem, asserts her love for the Lord. She rejects the idea of worshipping various gods and deities, as also of undertaking pilgrimages and holy baths. She longs only to become a slave of the Lord.

> I long only to be
> A slave, O Lord, at Thy feet;
> A slave indifferent
> Toward all except Thee.
>
> Of gods and goddesses I know not;
> Beloved Lord, without Thee
> I am ever distraught.
>
> In Ganga I won't take a bath,
> Nor rush to Jamuna for a dip;
> Holy Kashi I don't visit,
> Nor to Prayag make a trip.*
>
> Says Mira, dear Lord,
> Thee I long to meet,
> And I thirst only
> For Thy lotus feet.

MSS, p.815
Ban jaaoon charan ki daasi re

---

*A pilgrimage to the cities of Kashi (Varanasi) and Prayag is considered an act of great merit.

A Prayer

In this short prayer Mira invokes the Lord to ferry her across the terrible ocean of the world. She has taken His refuge and depends only on Him for her redemption.

> I have taken refuge in Thee, O Lord –
> Ferry me across as Thou deemest fit.
> Through all the holy places have I roamed,
> But never did my mind accept defeat.
>
> No one in this wide world is truly mine;
> Listen to my prayer, O Mighty One.
> Mira, Thy slave, depends only on Thee;
> From the noose of death, O Lord, release me.

MBP, p.224
Main to teri saran pari

The Master's Lotus Feet

Mira here gives expression to her love and longing for her Master. Having come to the feet of the Master, she has become impervious to the world and its attractions. Liberation is no problem for her now, since the Master's feet are the threshold of salvation.

> I am smitten with a longing
> For the lotus feet of my Master.
> For the Master's lotus feet, aye,
> And for crossing this ocean deep.
>
> Nothing do I desire
> Except to be at his feet.
> The world with all its lures
> Seems to me but a dream.
>
> The world's dreadful ocean
> Has become dry for me.
> To swim across it
> Now worries me no more.
>
> Mira's almighty Lord!
> Her Master's shelter
> Is all she longs for.

MBP, p.235
Mohe laagi lagan guru charnan ki

A True Devotee

Devotees of the Lord have always suffered insult and torment at the hands of worldly people; Mira herself was no exception. In this poem she brings out the devotee's quality of forbearance. There are many sly persons who pose as devotees of the Lord. But Mira points out that a true devotee is impervious to the taunts of the world. As diamonds do not lose their lustre when hit by a hammer, true devotees, always absorbed in the Lord's love, remain unruffled by the attacks of the world.

> Let people insult and injure you;
> Remain firm in your devotion to the Lord.
> The pure ones exist along with the sly –
> Whom would you call a devotee?
> They alone are true devotees
> Who calmly bear the world's taunts and blows.
>
> How would you know a pure diamond
> When it is mixed with stones
> Of the same shape and hue?
> That alone is the real diamond
> Which loses no lustre at the hammer's blow.
> Such a devotee, O Mira, is rare to meet,
> In whose heart forever dwell the Lord's feet.

MSS, p.403
Koi kahe tene kaheva re daeese

The Insane

Devotees and lovers of the Lord are looked upon by worldly people as mad. They are absorbed in the Lord's love and people cannot comprehend their inner state of bliss. Mira says that the Lord Himself looks after such lovers and performs all their tasks. She concludes that to attain such deep love for the Lord is the object of human birth, and if this is achieved nothing else remains to be done.

Mad? Yes, I am insane.
But the love of my Lord
Through madness I gained.

All through the ages past,
Of truth I was unaware;
My mind remained bound
By maya's vicious snare.

I was tossing about
In the world's stormy sea,
When through the storm, the Lord
Himself came unto me.

I am, indeed, insane
In the Lord's love; though
The joy of my madness,
Can the world ever know?

The bliss for which in vain
Even gods and angels pray –
In that bliss this mad one
Does revel night and day.

God alone in His love
Turned me mad, I am sure;
And through love's frenzy
Made me bright and pure.

People keep branding me
As mad, time and again;
But ever the Lord performs
All tasks of those insane.

The pleasures of the world
The mad find full of pain;
Can such lovers ever die?
Beyond death they remain.

This mad one in her craze,
Nothing else does she know,
Save to love and serve the Saints,
And at their feet to bow.

The love of her dear Lord,
In madness has Mira gained –
Nothing remains to be done;
Her object she has attained.

MSS, p.483
Ghelaan ame ghelaan-re

The Mighty Oak

When a person takes the first step on the path of divine love, people commend and admire him. But soon, in the words of Mira, the tiny seed of devotion sprouts and develops into a mighty tree. Then the devotee's only concern and thought is for the Lord, the object of his love. The traditional ways of worship, rituals and ceremonies no longer have any meaning for him, nor do worldly pursuits hold any attraction. People now start criticizing and deriding the devotee. This was Mira's lot in life. But she is not bothered by what people say. She cannot retrace her steps even if she tried to, for she is now in sight of her goal.

> When first I ventured on the path of love,
> No one tried to warn or hinder me;
> Now my love has taken root and grown,
> Like the tiny seed that grows into an oak.

> There is no question of retreat now;
> I am getting glimpses of the opposite shore.
> If I falter now, I'll be forever lost;
> The tightrope walker's one slip may cost his life.

> It is hard to unfasten a wet knot;
> Thus my mind is set in repeating His Name.
> I did try to free myself from the bond of His love,
> But my efforts failed; I have to endure the pain.

> In every household people deride me;
> Everyone has his own tale to tell;
> Each rattling pot has a bit to add.
> All fear and bow to public opinion,
> But I have discarded such cares as chaff.

An elephant carefree roams away from its herd;
Thus intoxicated with love I revel in joy.
Mira, Thy slave, has in her heart enshrined
The ambrosia of Thy devotion, O Lord.

MSS, p.377
Govind soon preet karat

Swan of the Crystal Lake

At one time the soul was enjoying bliss in her original home, but having come to the world, she has become involved in it and gathered dross around herself. Mira brings out this point through the imagery of a swan which, leaving the waters of the crystal lake (Mansarovar), comes and stays in a dirty pond.

Without the Lord, to me
This township appears
Desolate and dreary.

The swan whose repast once
Was shining pearls divine
Now after millet runs.

Leaving the crystal lake
Of bliss that was his home,
He has now come to take
Abode in a muddy pond.

His plumage once sublime
Is now smeared with slime.

Soon the pond will be dry,
And then it will be time
For him to leave, and fly.

Mira's dear Lord, when
Will you your arm extend,
And with much love and grace
Take her in your embrace?

MBP, p.185
Maadho bina basti ujaar

External Observances

Mira calls upon her fellow human beings to adopt the path of love and devotion in order to attain the Lord. Life is short and fleeting; it should not be wasted in futile external practices. Mira says that the Lord cannot be attained by renouncing the world, by adopting the life of a mendicant or by becoming a recluse. Holy baths, pilgrimages and fasts are of no use. Such external observances and practices will not release one from his bonds; he will again have to return to this world.

> O my mind, adore the lotus feet
> Of the Lord, eternal and kind.
>
> The earth, the heavens and between,
> All that exists, beings great and small,
> Will one day perish and depart.
> From fasts and holy baths
> What will you gain?
> Even with Kashi's saw*
> You'll remain within bondage.
> Do not be vain of your body;
> To dust it will turn.

---

*In medieval times there was a large saw placed in the holy city of Kashi (Varanasi). It was believed that those who got themselves cut by this saw and thus sacrificed their life would attain liberation.

The world's like the bird's short-lived play
That ends with the end of day.
What use donning saffron robes?
What value the life of a recluse
Who gives up family and to forest turns,
Or who becomes a yogi, but never learns
The true way to the Lord?
This rare chance he loses,
And again to the world he returns.

Thy feeble slave Mira entreats Thee:
Mighty Lord, cut asunder
The noose of Yama.*
Pray, make me free.

MBP, p.160
Bhaj man charan kanval abinaasi

---

* The lord of death.

A Profound Truth

In this poem Mira points out that devotion to a living Master is more fruitful than external observances, austerities and pilgrimages. She says that this profound truth, this secret of God-realization, was imparted to her by her Master.

> My Master to me did impart
> This profound secret, O Lord:
> All merits of telling beads,
> Pilgrimage and austerities,
> And boons* for which the world does vie
> At the Master's lotus feet do lie.
>
> Love me, O Beloved, I pray;
> Within my temple ever stay.†
> To my countless faults pay no heed,
> Nor to my caste, colour or creed.
>
> O Lord, Mira begs to remind:
> Thou art gracious, mighty and kind;
> When angels of death make their raid,
> Come, dear Lord, come to Mira's aid.

MSS, p.335
Guru ye kahiun karan maan

---

* The four *padarth*: *dharma* (piety), *arth* (wealth), *kam* (fulfillment of desires) and *moksha* (salvation), the four boons that all Hindus are enjoined to strive to attain.
† The human body has been described by Saints as the temple of God.

The Bond of Love

This is another song in which Mira expresses her deep love for the Lord. She illustrates the strength and intensity of her love through examples from nature, and requests the Beloved to reciprocate her love.

How can the bond of my love for you break?
Like the diamond unyielding to the hammer's blow,
My love for you remains unshaken, O Lord.

As gold becomes one with *suhaaga*,*
So has my heart become attached to you.
As the lotus stalk lives within the water,
So do I ever dwell in you, O Lord.

As the moonbird looks, absorbed, at the moon,†
So have I lost my heart to you, O Lord.
As Mira adores you, O Beloved,
Pray, Thou too love and meet her, my Lord.

MSS, p.398
Hamare raure laagali kaise

---

* Borax or the salt of boron. It is used for purifying gold and for bringing out its lustre. In folklore it is believed that borax in the process becomes one with gold.
† The moonbird or chakor, a bird in folklore which is so much in love with the moon that it cranes its neck to keep its eyes fixed on the moon throughout the night.

The Divine Washerman

Mira compares the Master to a washerman who cleanses the disciple's mind of all its dross. With the soap of remembrance of the Lord and the water of divine love, the adept washerman scrubs off all the blemishes of the mind. Once the disciple's mind is thus washed by the Master, it will never again gather dirt and will become fit for the repetition of the Lord's Name.

> If Master, the washerman, washes your mind,
> It will never be soiled again.
>
> Break the chains of attachment, O fool,
> And transcend the bondage of your body.
> Annihilate the five and the twenty-five;*
> Kindle the lamp of your temple within.
>
> With remembrance as the soap
> And love as the water,
> Your mind, cleansed of all blemish,
> With virtue will shine.
>
> So deftly will the washerman scrub it clean,
> Even a speck of dirt it shall not gather again.

---

* The 'five' refers to the five passions (lust, anger, greed, attachment, and ego); the 'twenty-five' refers to the twenty-five prakritis (the five manifestations of each of the five elements of the human body).

In the body's cage your mind is a parrot;
Let it repeat the glory of the Lord's Name.

Mira is lost in the thoughts of her Lord,
For life in this world is a fleeting dream.

MSS, p.750
Dhoyan na maila hoy

In the Lord's Will

This poem brings out the spirit of surrender to the Lord that a devotee must inculcate within himself. Mira says that her only occupation is to remain engrossed in the thoughts of her Beloved. Having abandoned herself to His will, she will now live in the world as and how He wants her to.

> To the Lord's abode I will go,
> For He alone is my true love.
> I'll gaze upon His charming face
> And ever remain enthralled.
>
> In the calm of the night
> I will arise and go to Him,
> And return at dawn.
> Night and day I'll remain engrossed
> In communion with my Lord.
>
> I am ever anxious to please Him;
> Whatever clothes He will give me,
> I will gladly adorn myself with.
> Whatever He will give me to eat,
> For me will be a feast.
>
> My love for Him is ages old;
> Without Him even for a moment
> I will not be able to breathe.
> Wherever He wants me to stay,
> There with pleasure I'll abide.
> If He would want to sell me,
> Willingly I would be sold.

Beloved Lord of Mira,
Thou alone art almighty;
She takes refuge at Thy feet
And abandons herself to Thee.

MSS, p.379
Main to girdhar ke ghar jaaoon

My Eternal Companion

This poem expresses Mira's longing for the Lord. She likens her mind to a rogue elephant and entreats her Master to tame it so that she may pray to the Lord in peace and tranquillity.

My companion of life and death,
I cannot forget Thee day or night.
Without seeing Thee I am restless,
My heart alone knows my agony.

I climb high and gaze at the path
For Thee to come;
I long for Thee, I weep,
My aching eyes are red.

This entire world is false –
False is family, false are friends.
Lord, with folded hands I beg,
Heed my prayer and come.

My mind is like a rogue elephant,
Wilful, wicked and wild.
Place thy hand on my head like a goad,
O Master, and tame this wayward mind.

I long to look at Thy graceful form,
To gaze and gaze and be in ecstasy.
Thou alone art my God, O beloved Lord;
Mira remains ever absorbed in Thee.

MSS, p.167
Mhaare janam-maran ra saathi

A Sound Bargain

In reply to the remonstrances of her family members, Mira says that she has struck a rare bargain in purchasing the Priceless One. Others feel that Mira has made a blunder in giving herself up completely to the path of devotion. But Mira revels in this profitable deal.

> O mother, I have purchased the Lord.
> Some say I have bought Him in secret,
>   some say by stealth;
> But no, I have got Him openly,
>   to the beat of a drum.
>
> Some say I paid a high price,
> Some say I got Him cheap;
> But I bought after weighing Him well.
>
> Some say He is dark and sombre,
> Some claim He is fair and bright;
> Him, the Priceless One, have I bought.
>
> This all the world knows well,
> With open eyes I have bought Him.
> Pray grant Thy vision to Mira, O Lord,
> And redeem Thy promise of ages past.

MBP, p.183
Maa'i ri main to leeno govindo mol

Smitten by Love

The Lotus-eyed One has smitten Mira's heart with His beauty and charming ways. Now she is feeling the pangs of separation and is restless. She knows that the Beloved is not far, for He resides within the human body. Yet, unable to see Him, she prays to Him to come and meet her without delay.

> The One with lotus eyes has, O mother,
> Entrapped my heart by His charming ways.
> He pierced it with a sharp arrow,
> Then left me and went far away, O mother.
>
> When the dart entered, I felt no pain;
> Now, O mother, I cannot bear it.
>
> Magic herbs and potions have I tried;
> Nothing could ease my anguish.
> Is there anyone – anyone merciful
> Who can allay my suffering, O mother?
>
> Thou art not far, near art Thou;
> Tarry not, Lord, come meet me.
>
> The fire of my burning heart, pray quench,
> For Thou with lotus eyes my heart did wrench.

MBP, p.174
Man hamaara baandhyo maa'i

---

*This poem of Mira is also found in some earlier editions of the Adi Granth.

Mira's Eternal Consort

After drifting endlessly in the dreadful ocean of transmigration, Mira, at the feet of her Master, has realized the Lord. In her ecstasy, she says that she is now wedded to the One who is eternal and almighty.

> I am wedded to the Immortal One,
> O friend; the Eternal One is my spouse.
>
> Kinfolk love you for their selfish ends;
> From their bonds and snares
> I have freed myself.
> Birth in this world has been a great torment;
> It kept me involved in futile pursuits.
>
> The entire world is dreadful and dark –
> I realize it, and I shudder in fear.
> In this vale of tears I suffered much pain
> And kept on wandering in the eighty-four.
>
> Great is my joy in the Saints' company –
> My roving has ended, I rest in peace.
> By the grace of my true Master,
> I was carried across the terrible sea.
>
> Mira, in refuge at her Master's feet,
> Sings the glory of her eternal Lord.

MSS, p.384
Akhand var ne vari saheli

The Spinning Wheel

There was a time when practically every woman in Rajasthan knew how to spin yarn on a *charkha*, a small hand-operated spinning wheel. In this poem Mira says that her spinning wheel—the human body—has been fabricated by the skilled Artisan. She would control her wayward mind to make it the belt or band to smoothly turn the wheel. Normally, the five senses are plying the spinning wheel; that is, the body and mind are completely under their control. Mira calls them five close friends who are pulling the yarn downwards, the wrong way. The yarn has to be stretched up vertically in order to spin it strong and fine. An adept spinner draws the yarn vertically, raising her hand skywards. Mira says that the realized soul—the 'married woman'—is an expert spinner, for she draws the yarn up to the firmament of the spiritual regions within.

Concluding the poem, Mira praises her Master who, like an expert tradesman, has sold her product in the highest market and obtained for her the treasure of Nam in return.

> How am I to ply the spinning wheel?
> The belt on the pivot finds no hold;
> It slips off again and again, my mother.
> Even so my life keeps slipping
> Without the support of my dear Lord.
>
> The adept Craftsman has made
> This spinning wheel for me.
> I'll make my wayward mind
> The belt, to run the spinning wheel.

Love is the carder who, with great care,
Has cleansed and carded my cotton;
On the pallet of knowledge it is rolled.

My five confidantes assemble to spin,
But they keep pulling the yarn the wrong way.
The fortunate soul, the wedded one,
Is the deft spinner who has the skill.
She alone spins the yarn with ease
And stretches it up to Gagan.*

The finished product,
The yarn of divine knowledge,
Reaches the best market
And fetches a high price.
My Master is an adept tradesman;
He bartered my yarn
For a priceless article.

Says Mira, O beloved Lord,
In bliss and ecstasy,
I look at my Master
And sing his glory.

MSS, p.757
Renttia ne kis vidh kaatun e maay

---

* The sky of the second spiritual region in the soul's journey within.

Above Slander and Praise

Mira was much criticized by the orthodox priestly class for her total disregard of the traditional methods of worship. The King of Mewar and members of Mira's family were particularly annoyed with her for adopting a cobbler, Sant Ravidas, as her Master. In this poem she tells her critics that, unmoved by their praise or slander, she will not abandon the chosen path nor be untrue to her Master.

Slander me to your heart's fill, O people!
But rust can never gather on gold.

Seeing all the world go flitting by,
To worship God I chose this spiritual path.
If now I err in my devotion,
I would bring disgrace to my Master.

I hail your achievement, O people;
An ant you have turned into an elephant.
Without seeing with your own eyes,
Without ascertaining the truth,
You have built fables in the air.

I have dismissed pride in my lineage;
I have broken all the ties of my family.
All bonds of attachment have I sundered;
I have given up all claims to the world.

All fondness for praise have I discarded;
Beyond the two* do I rest in peace.
You may tell your tales as you please.
Mira ever sings praises of the Lord,
And unmoved she bears the censure of all.

MBP, p.125
Ninda mhaari bhalaa'i karonai

---

* Praise and slander.

The Master's Grace

This short poem expresses the devotee's joy at meeting the Master within. Mira points out that it is through the grace of the Master that the Lord is realized.

> My heart is filled with joy;
> In an instant the dear one
> Appeared before me.
> I met the Beloved and through His grace
> The Lord revealed Himself to me.
>
> The Master joined me with Shabd, my source,
> And I am absorbed in its sweet melody.
> Mira's Lord is ever loving and kind;
> The bliss of union has stilled her mind.

MBP, p.225
Main to raaji bha'i mere man men

Mira's Torment

Mira is distraught with the pain of separation from the Beloved. Her agony remains unabated and she feels as if her bed is laid on the gallows, where one can never have a moment's rest. She finds it impossible to meet the Beloved, for He dwells in the subtle inner regions, to which she is unable to ascend. Concluding the poem, Mira says that her ailment will end only when the Lord Himself comes to her as the healer.

> O friend, in love I am insane;
> None knows my suffering, nor my pain.
>
> On the gallows is laid my bed;
> How can I get a moment's sleep?
> In the sky within is spread
> The couch of my Beloved;
> Access to Him how can I gain?
> O friend, in love I am insane;
> None knows my suffering, nor my pain.
>
> The wounded alone will know
> The anguish of the wounded,
> Or He who has dealt the blow.
> Only a *jauhar* with that zeal
> Will know what other *jauhars* feel,*
> Or she who has the inner bent.

---

* In Rajasthan, when a fort was besieged and the defenders realized that it could not be further defended under any circumstances, old people, pregnant women, children and the infirm were taken to safety through a secret passage; but the rest of the women remained behind with the men in the fort. The men would arm themselves, put on saffron-coloured robes and come to bid farewell to their wives. The women, bedecked in their wedding clothes and adorned with ornaments, would give a warm send-off to their husbands. They

O friend, in love I am insane;
None knows my suffering, nor my pain.

Like a wounded beast, vale to vale
I run in pain; I cannot endure.
No healer could I ever find
Who my constant agony could cure.

Then alone will I be rid of misery
When my Lord comes as the healer to me.
Mira in her love is insane;
None knows her suffering, nor her pain.

Mira, Vyaktitwa aur Kartritwa, p.271
He ri main to prem divaani

---

would also remind them that death in the battlefield is a glorious event and preferable to the disgrace of defeat. Immediately after the departure of their menfolk, they would prepare a huge pyre, and singing joyful songs of love and valour, enter it to be burnt to ashes, while the menfolk fought to the end. This was known as *jauhar*.

It was believed that when husbands thus died in the battlefield defending their freedom, and wives in *jauhar*, they would meet in heaven and live together blissfully. Rajput women looked upon such a death as a matter of great honour and glory and would mount the pyre with a fervour hard to describe or understand. Such a *jauhar* took place a few months after Mira left Chittor, in which legend says that over ten thousand women entered the pyre.

Mira here conveys the intensity of her longing for the Lord by alluding to the zeal of the *jauhar* (a woman who commits *jauhar*), who burns herself alive in order to meet her beloved husband in the next world.

The word *jauhar* in this poem has usually been translated 'jeweller' by scholars. Taking 'jeweller' as the meaning the lines would read: "Who else but a jeweller / will appreciate the jeweller's skill / or he who has the talent." The idea of the jeweller's aptitude or skill in judging the worth of a gem does not, however, convey the deep pain and intense longing that is the central theme of this poem.

Forsake Not, O Master

In this poem Mira expresses the devotee's faith in the Master, who is her lord and saviour. She prays to the Master to rescue her from the torment of birth and rebirth in this world.

> Forsake me not, kind Master!
> I am a feeble woman,
> Helpless and devoid of strength;
> Forsake me not.
> You alone are my shelter, O lord.
>
> I have no merits;
> Full of faults am I.
> You alone are faultless and powerful.
> I belong only to you.
> Where else can I find shelter
> Except at your feet?
>
> You alone are the jewel of my heart;
> You alone are Mira's lord.
> Except you she knows no other saviour.
> Pray save her
> From the further humiliation
> Of return to this world.

MSS, p.322
Chhorr mat jaajyo ji mahaaraaj

A Rare Boon

Human birth is a rare privilege given by the Lord to attain Him.
But human beings, through indulgence in vain pursuits, lose this
chance, which they obtain after many births in the lower species.
Mira says that one should make the best use of the human birth
and cross the dismal ocean of this world.

This rare birth you may not get again.

Through past acts of merit and worth
You were granted the human birth.
From day to day in age you gain,
But with each moment life does wane.

When death comes nothing will stay;
This precious chance will slip away.
When once a leaf has broken free,
It cannot then rejoin the tree.

The world's ocean does roar and rage;
Vast and deep, it is hard to gauge.
Board the ship of Nam, cross the sea,
Reach the shore of bliss and be free.

The vast world in its fourfold frame
Is nothing but a *chausar* game.*
Deftly play the pawn of your soul,
And you win the match, attain the goal.
But if deceitfully you load the dice,
With human birth you pay the price.
Saints and sages, Masters kind,
Try to warn us, and remind
That life is but a brief sunshine;
Hence Mira longs for love divine.

MSS, p.747
Nahin aiso janam baarambaar

---

* *Chausar* or *chopar* (pachisi) is an Indian indoor game, played on a board (usually made of cloth) that has four folds. Each fold is divided into small squares. There is an additional large square in the centre of the board, called the 'home'. The pawns that reach 'home' do not come back on the board, and the player whose pawns reach 'home' first is the winner. The pawns move according to the count of the dice.

Here Mira likens the world to the *chausar* board, its four folds being the four yugas or ages through which the soul passes from life to life, like the pawn in the game moving from square to square according to the throw of the dice; that is, according to the karmas. The four folds of *chausar* are also likened by some Saints to the four *khanis* or classes of life in the world through which the soul passes in its rounds of birth and rebirth.

One Who Drinks Nectar

When an ordinary person gains access to the household of a king, all his needs are fulfilled. He does not have to crave for the petty things of life. Mira, taking this as an example, says that she has attained access to the abode of the Most High and consequently the cravings of her mind have vanished. Through a few illustrations, she brings out an important aspect of the path of the Saints: namely, it is only when one is attached to the Lord within that he naturally becomes detached from all else in the world. When a person has tasted the nectar of inner bliss, he automatically becomes averse to the rancid waters of the world.

> I have gained access to the Noble One's house;
> The cravings of my mind have now vanished.
>
> Lakes don't interest me, why would I go to a pond?
> I am not concerned with Ganga and Jamuna,
> For I desire to go and merge into the ocean.
>
> I have no business with servants;
> I deal neither with courtiers nor nobles,
> For with the King alone I converse.
>
> I care not for lead nor for iron;
> Neither gold nor silver do I fancy,
> For my wares now are jewels and diamonds.
>
> From its sleep my fortune has awakened,
> And I am bound for the ocean deep.
> Who would forego the cup of nectar
> For a drink of turbid water?

To Pipa* the Lord did reveal Himself,
Filling his coffer with the wealth of grace;
That very Lord Mira has met face to face.

MSS, p.397
Badde ghar taali laagi

---

* King Pipa, like Mira, was also a disciple of Saint Ravidas.

To Meet the Beloved

The imagery of this beautiful poem is typical of Mira. Like an Indian bride of medieval times who bedecks herself with flowers and jewels—but without the jingling ornaments that might draw the notice of others—and goes to meet her husband in the darkness of the night through desolate lanes, Mira goes to meet her Lord.

Divesting herself of the tinsel of family pride and honour, and fearless of public slander, she enters the narrow lane of divine knowledge. She has adorned herself with the ornaments of love and devotion, and in a sacred tray she is carrying simran as her present for the Beloved. Mira gives hints of her inner journey by describing the meeting place with her Beloved as the high tower beyond the three attributes,* and she refers to the five Melodies as the five-coloured canopy.

> There is no one who can hold Mira back;
> Lost in love, she marches firmly on her path.
> Family pride and fear of public opinion
> Are useless burdens I have cast aside.
> Honour and censure I've flung from my head,
> And I freely tread the lane of knowledge.
>
> In the high tower with the bright red gate,
> Beyond the three attributes is laid my bed.
> Its five-coloured canopy brightly shines
> With clusters of flowers in glorious bloom.

---

* Harmony, action and inertia.

I'm adorned with ornaments bright and rare;
My forehead glows with the mark of vermilion.*

My hands lovingly hold the salver of simran;
Thus am I bedecked and my radiance grows.
In this benign and blissful hour today,
On the couch of *sukhmana*† does Mira stay.

To thy palace, O Rana, pray retreat;
Our paths diverge, they can never meet.

MSS, p.390
Tero koi nahin rokanahaar

---

* A mark made on the forehead by Indian women with a powder of vermilion colour. It is regarded as auspicious and is put on the foreheads only of married women. Here Mira hints at the opening of the eye centre and the inner light that the devotee sees within.

† *Sukhmana* is not to be confused with the *sushumna* of the yogis, which is the central canal along the spine. The central path, starting from the eye centre and leading upwards to the higher spiritual regions, has been called *sukhman* or *sukhmana* by the Saints. In this poem, the reference is clearly to the central path in the inner spiritual regions.

The Intoxication of Love

Mira is intoxicated with the wine of divine love. In a subtle manner she identifies love with Shabd or the Word, which has the qualities of bright light and the sound of thunder. The Master has removed the veil of delusion from her eyes and now she sees the one Lord present in all beings. She is intent on ascending to the realm of the Inaccessible One, which she describes as the tower of Agam.[*]

> I am intoxicated by the Lord's love.
> His love like a soft rain around me
> Saturates my every pore with bliss.
> Brilliant lightning surrounds me
> With its deep and thunderous roar.
>
> Breaking the barriers of delusion,
> My Satguru unfolded this mystery –
> The One Soul fills all vessels
> Yet remains apart from all.
>
> Now I will light the torch of true knowledge
> And will firmly climb to Agam's tower.
> Mira, ever a slave of her dear Lord,
> Craves to lay her all at His feet.

MSS, p.842
Laagi mohin raam khumaari ho

---

[*] The Inaccessible.

An Invocation to the Master

Mira prays to her Master to take her under his shelter, overlook her shortcomings and give her the blessings of his company. The Master alone can turn the devotee's attention towards the Lord. Mira implores him to do so.

Pray take care of me as you deem fit.

I await you with each blink of my eyes;
Please come, I long for a glimpse of your face.
There's no end to my failings and faults;
Take not my shortcomings to heart.
I am a slave even of your slaves;
My Lord, after union, don't part.

Mira longs to remain
In your shelter, O Master.
Turn all her attention
To the feet of the Lord.

MBP, p.193
Mhaari sudh jyoon jaano jyoon leejo ji

Longing for the Lord

The tenth door, or the third eye, has been opened. The soul now shines in its own resplendence. It beholds the dazzling light of the inner spiritual regions and desires to proceed to greater heights. Mira points out that it is only when the soul vacates the nine portals of the body and goes within that it develops a true longing to meet the Lord.

> I am struck with longing to meet the Lord –
> To meet the Dear One and reach my true home.
> Worldly entanglements and fear of slander
> I'll give up in pursuit of true knowledge.
>
> The door* is unlocked, my soul shines bright
> And longs for the mansion within the sky.
> A dazzling flame appears before me,
> Like a flash of lightning in days of rain.†
>
> Mira yearns now to behold her dear Lord
> And sing His glory in blissful ecstasy.

MSS, p.381
Mujhe lagan lagi prabhu paavan ki

---

* The tenth door behind the two eyes; the third eye.
† The dazzling flame and lightning refer to the light in the first spiritual region on the soul's inner journey.

Nam My Only Possession

Mira declares that the Lord's Name is her only belonging in this world. Through the association of Saints she is rid of all worldly bonds and has realized her oneness with the Lord.

The Lord's Name is all that I own;
Nothing else belongs to me.

I have given up my father,
Given up mother and brother,
Given up all that were once
Close to my heart.
Through the company of Saints
I am rid of the fear of public opinion.
To meet the Saints I rush with joy;
A look at the worldly gives me pain.

With the stream of my tears
I have watered love's everlasting vine.
In my life I met two *saviours* –
The Saint and the Lord's Name.
The Saint ever adorns my forehead;
The Name is embedded in my heart.
I took the essence of the ultimate truth,
And to me the mystery unfolded –
'I am He' and 'He is me'.

The Rana sent a cup of poison;
Cheerfully I sipped it,
And I am drunk with the wine
Of divine ecstasy.

My love is not a secret any more;
People all around know it.
Mira, the Lord's slave, is carefree;
Let happen whatever has to be.

MSS, p.410
Ab to mera raam naam

Light Thy Temple

In this poem the human body is compared to a temple in which one must light the lamp of divine knowledge before it is too late. But most people, after wasting their entire life in vain pursuits, expect to realize the Lord at the time of death. Mira warns that in old age the temple of the body starts shaking, the flesh and muscles waste away, only brittle bones, like tottering pillars, remain. Even the foundation, that is 'the life force', is about to give way. The end has come.

It is now that a person wants to light the lamp of knowledge, but having made no provision for oil he goes in search of it from door to door; in other words, he involves himself in external observances. It is, however, too late. The life force that was running the show has been withdrawn and the shop of the body is now vacant. The *yamdoots*, or the messengers of death, rejoice for they have yet another soul in their clutches.

Mira concludes the poem by suggesting that those who, like her, have attained the Lord while still living effortlessly drive away the messengers of death.

> Your temple without the lamp
> Is dark and dismal.
> The chapel is now shaking,
> Ready to topple.
>
> Its pillars, wasted with age,
> Now stand frail and old,
> And the sinking foundation
> Their weight cannot hold.

With cup in hand one goes
Door to door for oil,
That the lamp he may kindle,
But vain is his toil.

The grocer has quit his stall,
The shop is empty,
And the minions of Yama
Are dancing with glee.

But Mira in the Lord's love
Does happily stay;
The serfs of Yama, with ease,
She drives away.

MSS, p.754
Mandiria men deevadda binaanun andhaaroon

Satsang

Mira urges everyone to seek the company of Saints. All the scriptures and holy books, she says, have extolled the virtues of satsang, which leads to salvation. It is through the company of Saints that a person can acquire divine qualities and true devotion for the Lord.

Taste the nectar of satsang, O friend;
Oh, savour the elixir of satsang.
At the outset it tastes sharp and acrid,
But soon, like mango, it is juicy and sweet.

Do not be vain of your body;
It will one day be reduced to dust.
Elephants, steeds and your hoard of wealth
Will not go with you at the time of death.

In minutes satsang will lead to salvation;
Thus avow the Vedas and all holy books.

Says Mira, let the virtues of the Lord
And His lotus feet dwell within your heart.

MSS, p.772
Satsang no ras chaakh praani

My Eyes Ache

This poem typifies Mira's intense love for the Lord. The sweetness of His voice, the pangs of separation and her long nights of loneliness are blended in this song of tears.

Without seeing Thee my eyes burn and ache.
Since the time I was parted from Thee, O Lord,
Never did I have a moment's respite.
When I listen to Thy Word, my heart throbs;
Sweet, indeed, as nectar is Thy Voice.

With unblinking eyes I look at Thy path;
Each night without Thee is like months to me.

To whom shall I tell the woes of separation?
A saw has cut through my heart, O friend.

Thou conferrer of joy, Thou destroyer of pain,
When wilt Thou meet me, O Lord of Mira, again?

MBP, p.110
Daras bin dookhan laage

128

Divine Wedding

God-realization has been termed by Mira the 'soul's wedding'. When the newly wed soul meets other souls in the Lord's abode, they ask her why she remained unmarried for such a long time. The soul's reply is significant; she remained unmarried because all through the eons she did not meet a true Master, who alone could find the groom, arrange the wedding and give away the bride. In other words, union with the Lord cannot be attained except through a true Master.

Mira goes on to describe the marriage ceremony by referring to the formalities of a typical Indian wedding. The father of the girl finds a suitable match for her and chooses an auspicious time for the ceremony; a wedding canopy is set up and decorated with frills and flowers, under which he gives away the bride by placing her hand in that of the groom. He gives her a dowry of clothes and jewellery, which must include a necklace. The daughter then bids farewell to aunts, uncles, sisters and other relatives and accompanies her husband to the music of drums and other instruments.

Mira says that it was the Master who found the divine Bridegroom for her, selected the auspicious moment for the wedding, set up the wedding canopy in the inner regions, decorated it with esoteric jewels, and taking her, the bride, along with him, placed her hand into that of her Bridegroom—the Lord. As a dowry he gave the clothes of virtue, the jewels of love and true knowledge, and the priceless necklace of Nam, the Name of the Lord.

> "You are blessed, O soul, you are now married,
> But why so long a maid's life did you lead?"
>
> Until now I met not the Master kind;
> Who else for me, O friend, a match could find?

The very moment my Master I met,
He found the Groom and the wedding was set.
At an hour auspicious and benign,
He fixed my nuptials with the Groom Divine.

The wedding spire He built beyond the sky;
Its beauty and sparkle no jewels could vie.
My hand in that of the Groom did He place;
Thus I was wedded through my Master's grace.

My Master gave in dowry gifts so rare –
Jewels of virtue, the boon of love as my share,
The ornament of knowledge so fine,
And the priceless necklace of Nam Divine.

I've left uncles,* aunts† and their lure behind,
And tossed the ten sisters‡ out of my mind.
To the playmates§ I've bid my last farewell;
Now in my Master's company do I dwell.
I had remained with my parents for long;
Now I've left to the sound of drum and gong.
To my true home blithely I climb;
Beyond the darkness is that Being Sublime,
Who is One, who is the Essence Divine.

---

* The five passions.
† Worldly desires and cravings.
‡ The ten senses: five of action and five of perception.
§ The twenty-five prakritis.

In truth 'twas for Him that Mira did pine;
Now I'm His bride, He the dear Groom of mine.

Until now I met not the Master kind;
Who else for me, O friend, a match could find?

MSS, p.846
Surta savaagan naar kunvaari kyoon rahi

Clue to the Eternal Abode

In this poem Mira expresses her longing to return to her eternal home, from where all souls originally came. She could not find anyone who could unfold the mysteries of the mansions within and cure her of her pain of separation from the Lord. As a result, she continued to take birth in this world in various species. But when she met her Master, Saint Ravidas, the long spell of her sufferings ended, for he gave her the 'clue' or the way to reach her true home.

> Mira is now resolved to soar
> To the celestial skies within.
>
> Whenever I think of that home,
> My eyes fill with tears.
> In my longing I suffer
> With an ever-increasing pain.
> It hurts constantly;
> Hurts like an arrow
> That has pierced my heart,
> And I have become averse to food and drink.
> So intense is separation's pain
> That night after night I remain
> Restlessly awake.
>
> I long to meet that healer
> Who has fathomed the mysteries
> Of the lands and worlds within.
> Him alone will I tell of my ailment
> And forever be rid of this wandering
> From species to species,
> From birth to birth.

I kept searching for the secret
Of that realm, but none could reveal it.
When Saint Raidas, my Master, I met,
He gave my soul the clue to that eternal abode.
Then I ascended and met my Beloved,
And my anguish was finally allayed.
I looked upon the world as dust
And realized my own true home.

MBP, p.207
Meera man maani surat sail asmaani

The Path of Devotion

The path of devotion is not for the timid or the faint-hearted. The devotee must have firmness and courage and should step onto the path as a valiant warrior enters the battlefield. Like Sant Kabir and Sant Paltu, Mira also says that the devotee has to enter the lane of love without his head; that is, he must give up his ego or I-ness, he should adopt a spirit of humility and surrender, and should live in the will of the Lord.

Concluding the poem, Mira points out that time is fleeting; one should make the best use of this brief sojourn here by seeking the company of the Saints. They are the beloved sons and daughters of the Lord; they are beyond birth and death, beyond the fear and bondage of the world.

The Lord is my Beloved;
Apart from Him,
There is nothing
That exists for me.

Like a boat sailing
On the high seas,
The lures of the shore
Hold no charm for me.

My sisters, O my friends,
Devotion's path is hard;
It's not for the timid
Nor for the weak to take.

Only the brave tread
The path of devotion,
Forever on the march
But without their heads.*

To reach the Lord they
Rush into the field;
The brave ones wield
Their weapons with valour.

The cowards, faint of heart,
Take to flight in fear;
The valiant, ever firm,
Charge with all their might.

The caravan of the world,
O Mira, moves on;
Life here is fleeting,
A brief sojourn.

Eternal are the Saints,
To the Lord so dear –
Beyond all bonds,
Free from all fear.

MSS, p.775
Main olagyo raamaro

---

* Without any ego.

An Invocation

This is a typical song of Mira, based on a popular folk tune of Rajasthan. The first stanza, with slight modification, is repeated after every few lines as a refrain; otherwise, each stanza is self-contained. The sighs of Mira's longing for the Lord, however, echo throughout this song.

Come, pray come, O Lord of mine;
I await Thee, I long and pine.
Oh come to my mansion, come, I pray;
I stand with eyes glued on thy way.

I'll shed with the coming of the morn
All fineries that now me adorn.
On the path of life, forlorn I stand,
For Satguru* to come and hold my hand.

I hold a goblet of love for thee;
Oh come, my Master, hearken to me.

The Saint is my life, my soul is he;
He pervades within, he dwells in me.
In my every pore does he reside,
As does rain in the clouds abide.

My soul is attuned to Name Divine;
Oh come, pray come, dear Lord of mine.

---

*The true (*sat*) Master (*guru*).

136

Mira is the Lord's beloved now,
And, O Lord, her only love art Thou.
Mighty Lord, to Mira in Thy grace
Hasten to grant a glimpse of Thy face.
My attention in Nij Nam* does stay;
Come, dear Lord of mine, oh come, I pray.

Come, I beseech Thee, O Lord of mine;
Come, I await Thee, I long and pine.

MSS, p.207
Aajyo aajyo govinda mhaare

---

*Nij Nam, 'the Lord's own Name', a term used by the Saints to denote the Lord Himself.

The Wealth of Nam

In this poem Mira sings the praises of Nam or the Word and expresses her unbounded happiness on being blessed with this rare wealth by her Master. In the boat of Truth or Nam, with her Master as the adept boatman, she crosses with ease to the sunlit shore.

The jewel of Nam I have found;
Precious wealth have I obtained.
A rare gift did my Master bestow;
In his mercy he has made me his own.

My original treasure I have regained,
And am rid of all I had in the world.
It can neither be stolen nor squandered;
It keeps on increasing from day to day.

The boat of Truth I occupied,
With the true Master at the helm.
With ease I was ferried across
The deadly ocean of the world.

Mira in her joyful ecstasy
Sings the glory of her benign Lord.

Mirabai ki Shabdavali, p.24
Paayo ji maine naam ratan dhan paayo

Love

To bring home to her sister-in-law Udabai the intensity of the devotee's love for the Lord, Mira quotes the example of the fish, the deer and the moth.

O Uda, pray do not talk of love.
The fish is in love with water;
Separated, she gives up her life.
The deer so loves the music*
That readily he faces the hunter's blade.
The moth, ever in love with the flame,
With joy offers himself to it.
Mira is in love with her Master;
She has laid her heart at His feet.

MBP, p.10
Ari eri oodaan laagi ka naam na ley

---

*It is believed in Indian folklore that the deer is enamoured of the music of the *mardang* (also called *mridang*), a kind of drum or tambourine. The hunters play on the *mardang* in the forest and the deer, drawn by its love for the music, comes and places its head on the instrument, and is thus captured and killed.

None like the Lord

This song expresses Mira's longing for her Beloved, whom she blames for ignoring her and for not even casting a glance at her. While lovers of the Lord are legion, there is only one Beloved Mira can look to.

Just glance at me once, O Lord;
My eyes are ever fixed on Thee,
But Thou casteth not a look at me.
Oh, Thy heart is as hard as granite!

I only long for Thy loving glance;
Nothing else do I ask of Thee.

There is none like Thee for me, O Lord,
But to Thee, there are millions like me.

Motionless, I stand praying before Thee;
Thus have I waited till the break of dawn.

Thou everlasting Lord of Mira, grant my wish,
And I'll render my life as the price to Thee.

MSS, p.471
Tanak hari chitvauji mori or

Fish Thirsty in Water

Mira scorns the idea of finding God in pilgrimages and external observances, and says that the idea of finding God outside is as ridiculous as saying that a fish is thirsty in water. Through the path of *sahaj*,* Mira has gone within and realized the Lord.

> To hear that a fish is thirsty in water,
> I feel amused and am moved to laughter.
>
> People, without realizing their true selves,
> Roam now to Mathura, now to Kashi.[†]
> Renouncing all, they wander in quest of God;
> Defeated, they drift in the world's vast ocean.
>
> But Mira, through the path of *sahaj*,
> Has met her dear eternal Lord.

MBP, p.136
Paani men meen piyaasi

---

* Shabd Yoga, or the Yoga of the Sound Current, is also called the path of *sahaj yoga*; its first step is the withdrawal of the soul current from the body to the eye centre, leading ultimately to self-realization and God-realization.
† Two places of pilgrimage in India.

Awaken, O Lord

It was a custom in the royal families of Rajasthan to awaken the kings by singing to them. The household ladies and maidservants used to sing every morning, calling on the ruler to awake, as the day was about to dawn. This practice was also followed in temples, where devotees used to sing before the idols. Those songs were known as *prabhati*, or songs of the dawn. They were set to such classical tunes as were considered suitable for the morning hours.

Mira has composed some poems in the *prabhati* style, but the burden of such compositions is love and longing. Here, she calls upon her emperor, the Lord, to awaken to her suffering and bless her with a sight of Him.

> Awaken, my Lord, the Emperor of all;
> Why don't you smile and speak to me?
> You reside forever within my heart;
> Why don't you lift the veil, O Lord?
>
> My body, mind and soul for you I adorn,
> And I lay my head at your lotus feet.
> Wheresoever I feel your presence, O Lord,
> There will I render humble service to you.
>
> To you I sacrifice my entire being;
> To you I dedicate myself forever.
> For your sake I have, O Lord,
> Set aside all family decorum.[*]

---

[*] Conventional behaviour of a member of the royal family.

Even though my message is brief,
Pray, know all that I fail to say.
I am your bondmaid, reared by you;
Have mercy, accept me as your own.

You alone are my merciful Lord;
Hearken to me, pray, tarry no more;
Mira, the slave at Thy feet,
Begs now for a sight of Thee.

MBP, p.77
Jaago mhaara jagpatiraa'i

The Way

Human birth provides the opportunity to worship the Lord and escape from the cycle of birth and death. But people do not know the way to worship God. Mira says that only one who is himself an adept in treading the path of true devotion can guide others. Being in constant touch with the Lord within, he can tell us about our true home.

It's my chance to worship the Lord,
But I know not the way of devotion.

One who is himself an adept on the path
Can, O friend, impart the secret to you.
He alone can enable you to hear
The message of the Inaccessible.

Do not plunge into the deep waters of the world,
But bathe with care at the edge.*
Be not lured by Maya's art and guile;
Instil the Lord's love deep within your heart.

Her Dear One's praises alone will Mira sing;
To His lotus feet within she'll ever cling.

MSS, p.753
Maare hari bhajyaani chhe vela re

---

*Through this analogy, Mira conveys that one should fulfil one's worldly obligations, but in a detached manner, not losing oneself in the affairs of the world.

The Springtime

Holi is India's spring festival, when people indulge in revelries. They spray coloured water and throw coloured powder at one another, and make merry by singing, beating drums and playing on cymbals.

In this poem Mira stresses the importance of human birth, which like the springtime is fleeting; Mira's Holi, however, is a Holi with a difference. The music that she enjoys is the music of the unstruck melody, and the colours she revels in are those of the spiritual regions within.* In this rapturous state she sacrifices her all at the feet of the Lord.

A nine days' wonder is the springtime;
It's your chance to play Holi, my mind.

Without cymbals, without drums,
The unstruck music comes resounding.
Without any tune, without any sound,
With no pause the Melody resounds,
Filling every pore of my body.

I fill love's spray with the hue
Of virtue and contentment,
And blissfully I sprinkle this colour around.
The colour scatters, the sky glows red,†
And without a stop it rains
In vivid and varied tints.

---

* In *Pathway to God in Hindi Literature* (1954, p.194), the well-known thinker and philosopher R. D. Ranade has described this poem as "a fine example of Mira's mystic experience of sound and colour".
† The allusion is to the light and sound of the second spiritual region within.

I have flung away the veil of my body;*
I have shed all reserve and fear
Of what people may say.
Such a Holi I play in this springtime.

Mira adores her beloved Lord;
She sacrifices her all at His lotus feet.

MSS, p.893
Phaagun ke din chaar

---

* The reference is to the withdrawal of the soul from the physical body to the
eye centre.

In Adoration

In this love song Mira says that she is charmed by the beauty of her Lord's eyes. She is absorbed in the bliss of the Beloved's company and now the objects of the world hold no attraction for her. She goes on to tell of the Master's greatness and her love for him. The idea of the unity between the Master and the Lord runs throughout this richly emotional poem.

> To my Beloved's charming eyes,
> My entire being I sacrifice.
> Them do I love, them I adore,
> Again and again, evermore.
>
> My dear Lord brought me to His heart;
> Not for a moment will I let Him part.
> Fondly to Him now I will cling;
> His praises with joy will I sing.
>
> To my Beloved's charming eyes,
> My entire being I sacrifice.
> Them do I love, them I adore,
> Again and again, evermore.
>
> Worldly pursuits have lost their lure;
> In love I'm mad, there is no cure.
> When Saints' presence I come to know,
> Joyfully there I hasten to go.
>
> To my Beloved's charming eyes,
> My entire being I sacrifice.
> Them do I love, them I adore,
> Again and again, evermore.

Ganga, Jamuna, are in my home;*
To holy sites why need I roam?†
Holiest of all, at the Saints' feet,
I daily bathe where three streams meet.‡

To my Beloved's charming eyes,
My entire being I sacrifice.
Them do I love, them I adore,
Again and again, evermore.

On the eleventh§ why need I fast?
Three times a day I take repast.
Mira in His love's sunshine
Drinks the Nectar of bliss divine.

To my Beloved's charming eyes,
My entire being I sacrifice.
Them do I love, them I adore,
Again and again, evermore.

MSS, p.515
Maara naathana nainaan oopar re

---

* Here Mira refers to the human body as the home.

† The 'holy sites' are the sixty-eight places of pilgrimage in India; a visit to these places and a bath there is believed to wash away sins.

‡ Mira here uses the word Tribeni. She hints at the Radiant Form of the Master, which is met within at a place described by the Saints as Tribeni—'the confluence of three Streams'. The outer Tribeni is the confluence of the three rivers Ganga, Jamuna and Saraswati at Allahabad; a bath at this place is regarded as a holy act. Mira says that she daily goes within and bathes at the true Tribeni, which is at the Master's feet in the inner regions.

§ Ekadasi, the eleventh day; a fast on the eleventh day of the new moon is considered to be a pious act.

A Rare Chance

Mira calls upon us to realize the importance of human birth—a rare chance to attain the Lord. She goes on to say that she has met her Master and realized the Truth through his grace. It is only the valiant who surrender their entire being at the feet of their Master, go within and drink the nectar of divine realization.

Human birth is a rare jewel
You have obtained;
It is a blessing
You may not get again.

Now is your chance to acquire Knowledge;
Now is your chance to repeat the Lord's Name.
I have met the Master
And through his grace
I have realized the Truth;
In my Master I have recognized the Lord.

The valiant, who take the Master's shelter,
Drink to their fill the Nectar within;
They who have no Master go thirsty.

My mind is now engrossed in bliss,
And I sing the praises of the Lord.

I have met a Master primal and eternal;
Without him I would have continued
Whirling in the vast ocean of the world.

Says Mira, I am wary of people;
O Master, now only to thee
I look for grace and mercy.

MSS, p.847
Manakha janam padaarath paayo

The Lord and His Name

Mira begins this short poem by asserting her love for the Lord's Name. In the next few lines she says that her charming Beloved has entered her heart, thereby conveying the identity of the Lord with His Name. Persian and Indian mystics often say that there is no difference between the Nam and the Nami, between the Name and the Named One.

> I am attached to the Lord's Name;
> His Name alone I now love and cherish.
>
> My loving Friend has entered my heart
> As the string runs through a necklace.
> He is within all, yet ever apart;
> Not near, nor far, is the Mighty One.
>
> Mira now abides in the Lord's shelter;
> The fear of birth and death is set aside.

MSS, p.871
Hari naam se neh laagyo re

Longing for the Master

In this simple poem, Mira tells of her love and longing for the Master. Having taken his refuge, she has become his slave and craves only to be at his feet.

Come soon, my Master;
Thou art kind and merciful.
Come, and within my heart
Raise the harvest of joy.*

Separated from thee,
In agony and pain
Within my being,
I wither in anguish.

Like the lonely *koyal*,†
I sing sad tunes of longing;
Yet I fail to convey
The misery that remains
Buried within my heart.
The tigress of longing
Has made me her prey;
She's ruthlessly deaf
To my pleas for mercy.

---

* This is a phrase commonly used by women in Rajasthan. After one or two years' failure of crops, when the farmer starts planning for the next crop, the wife asks him to raise a harvest that will bring happiness to her suffering family.
† The Indian cuckoo; it is believed that it longs for the mango blossom.

Without seeing thee,
Beloved Master,
I writhe in anguish
Like a fish out of water.
Forlorn in the night,
For the dawn longs the *chakvi;*[*]
So do I, O Master,
For one glimpse of thee.

I await the flush
Of that glorious dawn,
When Thy loving presence
Will adorn my home.

O Master, thus begs
Mira, ever thy slave;
She only craves for the dust
Of thy lotus feet.

MBP, p.192
Mhaara satguru bega aajyoji

---

[*]An Indian waterbird which, according to folklore, is parted from its mate
during the night and therefore fervently longs for the daybreak.

Mira's Refrain

Mira longs to meet her beloved Lord. She is constantly repeating His Name and has become oblivious of herself and her surroundings. She compares her longing to a serpent that has bitten her heart, leaving her in constant agony. The only remedy is union with the Lord, for whom she is always yearning.

> My heart, O friend, aches
> To meet my beloved Lord.
> The shaft of longing has pierced me,
> And I writhe in the agony of separation.
> Day and night, with unblinking eyes
> I stare at the path for Him to come.
>
> 'Lord, O dear Lord!' is my only refrain;
> I am aware of nothing else.
> The asp of separation has stung my heart;
> Its poison is spreading in waves of pain.
> Beloved Lord, pray end my suffering;
> Come and meet me, do not delay.
> Fervent in her longing for the Beloved,
> Mira only craves for union with Him.

MBP, p.267
Raam milan ke kaaj sakhi

Without the Lord's Name

In this short poem Mira stresses the importance of the Name of
the Lord and the association with Saints for obtaining release
from the chain of birth and death. It is only by taking the shelter of
the Master that one can attain the bliss of union with the Lord.

> The soul without the Lord suffers in torment;
> Except Him, who can give her any solace?
>
> This world is truly a cauldron of evil;
> It likes not the company of the Saints.
> Always averse to the Lord's Name,
> It remains engrossed in actions good and bad.
>
> Without the Lord's Name no one can get release;
> He will continue to roam in the eighty-four.
> He never seeks the company of the Saints;
> The fool wastes the rare gift of human birth.
>
> Says Mira the slave,
> In the Master's refuge alone
> Can you attain supreme bliss.

MBP, p.240
Rama'iya bini yo jivarrau dukh paavai

The Adept Marksman

Sant Kabir, in one of his couplets, says that the Master shot him with the arrow of Shabd or the Word and he has become 'dead'. Mira, in this and the next poem, conveys the same thought. Her Master, a perfect marksman, has shot her with an arrow dipped in the fire of longing and she has become oblivious to her body and surroundings.

In contrast, the last three stanzas of this poem describe the Master as the skilled physician who has given Mira the panacea for all her worldly ills.

My Master has shot me with perfect aim,
With an arrow tempered in longing's flame.
My ears hear not, eyes fail to see
And legs are now of no avail to me.
I long for him, at the path I stare;
Of my stinging pain no one's aware.

So rare an herb did my Master give,
That calm and free from care I live.
Thus say the holy books: you'll not find
A true healer like the Master kind.
Now Mira will, with the Beloved roam
Blissfully in her eternal home.

MBP, p.161
Bhar maari re baana

In the same vein, Mira suggests in the second poem that longing for the Master has completely occupied her mind. Love for the Master has made it her captive, and it has now given up its habit of wandering about in the world.

> My Master with a poignant dart
> Pierced me right through the heart.
> The spear of longing has plunged deep;
> I remain restless and get no sleep.
>
> My mind has left its mercurial ways;
> Bound by the chain of love, quiet it stays.
> The one I adore alone does know
> The pain and torment that I undergo.
>
> What to do? Helplessly Mira bears
> The unrelenting surge of her tears.
> O Master, without meeting thee,
> Says Mira, there's no rest for me.

MBP, p.271
Ri mere paar nikas gaya

Pure as Gold

There is an autobiographical touch in this poem. Mira was averse to rites and rituals. She disregarded regal traditions and she loved the company of Saints. All these annoyed the Rana, the younger brother of her deceased husband, and when all efforts to change her failed, in sheer desperation he tried to poison her. Her faith was put to a severe test, but Mira came through the ordeal 'pure and bright'.

> You gave me poison, O Rana, I know.
> But freed of dross, like gold from the furnace,
> Did Mira emerge pure and bright.
>
> Public censure, decorum and rank
> I have tossed away like dirty water.
> Keep worrying about status and name;
> I, a feeble woman, am with love insane.
>
> The sharp arrow of love has pierced my heart;
> Deep it has gone, I am wild with pain.
> To the Saints I sacrifice body and soul,
> And their lotus feet I ever embrace.
>
> Mira's Lord, in mercy, saved her,
> Knowing her to be His own slave.

MBP, p.247
Raanaaji ten jahar diyo main jaani

The Obligation of the Path

Whenever the Lord comes in the human form as a Master, the devotees remind him that since he has donned the mantle of the saviour, he should maintain its glory and reputation by redeeming them in spite of all their faults.

In this poem, Mira reverses the image. Using the same terminology, she points out that once a seeker adopts the mantle of devotion, he also has to maintain its dignity. She says that it is easy to call oneself a devotee, but to maintain the obligation of devotion is no easy task. The devotee has to sacrifice his all and be prepared to face hardship and suffering with love and faith in the Lord. One can only tread the path to the Lord's abode with unfaltering steps, and poisons on the way have to be accepted as nectar.

> It is hard to maintain the dignity
> Of the mantle of devotion, O friend.
>
> Having donned the mantle, don't be vain;
> To attain salvation is no child's game.
> Prahlad* fulfilled this obligation
> When he faced his father's wrath,
> And on devotion's path remained steadfast.
>
> Once you enter the lane of devotion,
> Never look back, never a step retrace;
> Only thus you'll obtain the Lord's favour
> And ascend to His eternal abode.

---

*A devotee in Hindu mythology, Prahlad was the son of King Haranyakashyap, who was opposed to Prahlad's devotion to Lord Vishnu and constantly persecuted him. But Prahlad remained firm in his devotion.

Mira strived hard and attained
The boon of His love and devotion.
For His sake she endured, and never shrank –
When offered the cup of poison,
With trust in her Lord, she drank.

MSS, p.346
Baanaaro birrad duhelo re

A Prayer to the Master

This poem is a short prayer addressed by Mira to her Master, in separation from whom she is pining and suffering. A glimpse of the Master's face has bewitched her and now, day and night, she is longing to see him again.

Pray come, O Master, illumined and wise;
A glimpse of your face has enchanted me.
When you come my way, inquire for the one
Who, pining for you, is frenzied with pain.

Day and night I have no peace nor respite,
And I writhe like a fish out of water.
Save for your darshan nothing can soothe me;
In constant anguish, I'm nearing my end.

Mira is ever a slave at your feet;
Hear her prayer, O bestower of bliss.

MSS, p.843
Milta jaajyo ho guroogyaani

Wed the Unbegotten One

This is one of the many songs that Mira composed in the Gujarati language. It is set to a folk tune of Gujarat. The soul, having obtained the rare privilege of human birth, must strive to attain union with the Lord. As in some other poems, Mira has described God-realization as the soul's wedding with the groom who is unbegotten and unborn.

> Wed the Unborn Groom – it's your chance;
> At others never cast a glance.
>
> God gave you a gift of rare worth,
> This precious chance of human birth.
> Now why linger here, why tarry?
> The Unborn One must you marry.
>
> Some the Vedas, some scriptures read;
> Some split hairs, some argue and plead.
> Why between joy and pain be torn?
> Marry the Groom that ne'er was born.
>
> Put such bangles around your arm
> That never break nor come to harm,*
> Bangles the outer eye cannot see,
> Bangles of grace and of His mercy.
> Wed the Unbegotten Groom, O friend,
> Your heart to others never lend.
>
> Your being now with such a robe adorn
> That cannot be soiled, nor be torn.

---

*In orthodox Hindu families, married women wear bangles on both wrists. Breaking or damaging them is associated with bad luck.

With yarnless yarn it has been made,
And dyed in a hue that ne'er can fade.

O'er whom no birth nor death does loom,
Only Him you take as your Groom.

Nor shadows, nor a touch of pain,
Neither pleasures, nor sun nor rain,
Neither the world's fire, nor its fume,
Can ever touch it or consume.
In that primal and blissful clime,
Dwells your Unborn Groom Divine.
Wed the Unborn Groom – it's your chance;
At others never cast a glance.

Aboard the ship of Name Supreme,
Cross the sea, as you would a stream.
Reach the shore of bliss divine;
Bask with joy in love's sunshine.
Wed the Unborn Groom – it's your chance;
At others never cast a glance.

I sacrifice myself, Lord, to Thee;
Thou art the only succour for me –
Mira's life now with love adorn.
Marry the Groom that ne'er was born,
O'er whom no birth nor death does loom.
Only Him must you take as your Groom.

MSS, p.395
Anajaayo var variye re

Mira Firm in Her Devotion

A number of Mira's poems are in the form of a dialogue with her sister-in-law, Udabai, who had undertaken to 'reform' Mira and persuade her to give up the company of Saints. Mira, however, refuses to give in.

Mira:
Come what may, with love and devotion
I'll keep the company of Saints.
The Lord and His devotees are one –
The flower is not separate from its fragrance.
Merged are they in each other,
As butter is in milk.

Udabai:
O sister Mira, pray listen to me,
Renounce the company of Saints,
Bring not disgrace to our family.

Mira:
This path have I obtained with great difficulty;
My true Master has brought me to it.
In lieu of my head did I get it;
How can I ever let it go?

Udabai:
Born in a noble family,
Married into a princely one,
O fool, ignorant of thy rank,
Despise not the regal ways.

Mira:
Without devotion vain is all glory;
Uda, it holds no fascination for me.
Thrones and palaces are of no worth;
A day will come when they'll be reduced to dust.

Udabai:
People around the town berate thee,
They speak ill of thee,
They call thee names.
Family and kinsmen laugh;
They gather to mock and slander thee.

Mira:
Let them slander and defame me;
Cheerfully I will welcome it.
They cleanse me of my impurities,
Without soap and water.

Blessed and fortunate indeed is Mira,
For in the Lord's love her self she has lost.
To Him I look, to Him do I pray,
Whatever the people choose to say.

MSS, p.294
Mhe to karasyaanji preet lagaay

The Nectar of Nam

In this short poem Mira calls upon seekers to take to the company of Saints. She exhorts them to lead a pure life to enable them to partake of the elixir of Nam.

Drink the nectar of the Lord's Name;
My mind, drink the nectar of the Name Divine.
Forsake the company of the evil,
Sit at the feet of the Saints,
Listen to their accounts of the Lord.
Lust, anger, ego, greed, attachment,
Purge them all, and dye yourself deep
In the hue of Mira's dear Lord.

MBP, p.266
Raam Naam ras peeje manua

Divine Love

In this song Mira expresses her love and longing for the Lord. She would subdue the mind, free herself of the dross of the world and adorn her soul with the love of the Master. Love would be her tamboor, and to its beat she would sing and dance to please her Beloved.

The Lord's Name has taken abode within me;
Now I long only to please my winsome Lord.

I am hapless and forlorn,
My conduct is vile;
How can I fittingly sing His glory?
The strong bars of the cage of separation
I long to shatter, to be with Him.
Mind I will slay and of all dross be shorn;
My soul I'll adorn with Satguru's love.
With the cord of my soul and the loops of love,
I'll firmly fix the covering of the drum of Nam.*
With this drum of love, to its resounding beat,
I will repeat His praises in blissful tones.

With my body the cymbal and my mind the flute,
I'll awaken my soul from its sleep.
Thus before my Beloved will I dance in joy,
And forever become one with Him.

---

*The drumhead, made of leather, is stretched over the drum and held tight with loops and cord.

Lord, have mercy on this feeble one,
So she may ever chant Thy glory.

Beloved Lord, Thee alone Mira longs to meet;
Pray, bless her with the dust of Thy lotus feet.

MSS, p.869
Raam naam mere man basiyo

The Lord's Name

Whatever the people may say about her ways, Mira is firmly set on the path of devotion, which she describes as a sword's edge. The Word or Name has taken abode in her and she has merged herself into the Name.

Within me, O Lord, Thy Name has taken abode;
The world derides me because I adore Thee.

Some declare that Mira has gone insane,
Some say she is a blot on her family,
Some describe her as a raging fire,
But she is lost in her Beloved's Name.

A sword's edge is the path of devotion
With which I severed the noose of death.
Mira has known her beloved Lord
By merging in the ocean of Shabd.

MBP, p.216
Mere man raam naama basi

Sleep for Sale

Sleep is a great obstacle in the devotee's path. It overcomes him during the period of his spiritual practice, dissuades him from giving full time to meditation and, in general, makes him lethargic towards his spiritual pursuits. It even makes him indifferent towards his true objective.

For eons, the soul has remained oblivious of its true home and has, time and again, lost the rare privilege of human birth by keeping awake to the illusions of the world and remaining asleep to the spiritual treasure within.

In this unusual poem, Mira, employing the imagery of a weekly market of rural India, says that she will get rid of sleep by selling it off. Like the typical trader of the village market, she will secure a central and high place in the bazaar for her stall, and announcing the sale at the top of her voice, she will entreat the buyers to come. Without any compunction she will resort to the tricks usually employed by a sly trader: she will 'cheat' a customer by surreptitiously tipping the balance in the purchaser's favour or by stealthily placing more weight on her side of the scale in order to supply a larger measure of the commodity (sleep) at the settled price. Just as the village trader, with the approach of the evening, reduces his price to effect a quick sale of his remaining articles and return home, Mira offers to sell sleep at a price lower than the market rate in order to return home early.

Starting in a light, almost humorous vein, Mira concludes the poem on her usual tender note of love for the Lord.

> I will sell thee, O sleep,
> If a buyer I find.
> Sleep, my archenemy,
> I'll surely sell thee.

Even below the market rate
I will put thee on sale.
Two *paisa*[*] I'll charge
For a pound of thee;
Nay, half a *paisa*
For five pounds will do.
Even for a ton in weight,
Only a rupee I'll take.
I'll sell thee, O sleep,
For now I fully know
Thou art my most deadly foe.

"Sleep, oh sleep for sale!"
Loudly I'll shout and yell,
Begging the buyers to come.
If a customer approaches
With little money in his purse,
I'll dispose of thee on credit,
For payment at some distant date.
I will sell thee, my foe,
Below the market rate.

In the heart of the market
Will I set high my stall.
I will tip the balance
To give more of thee
Against a lesser weight.

---

[*] The smallest unit of Indian currency and almost worthless as a single unit.

If I can manage on the sly,
More weight will I add
To my side of the scale
And effect a rapid sale.
Thus will I sell thee,
O sleep, my enemy.

Sleeping on and on
Have I wasted my days.
For eons I have slept
And lost all my fortune.
Sleep, thou stubborn foe,
Pray go, make that home thy abode
Where devotees of my Lord
There are none.

My Beloved came home;
He left, for I, miserable one,
Remained lost in sleep.
Go hence, sleep, go;
All thy tricks I know.

Her dear Lord alone
Now Mira forever keeps
Softly entrapped
Within her eyes.
Depart thou, my enemy,
There is no room for thee.

Mirabai ka Jiwan-vritta evam Kavya, p.103
Neendarrli thaane bech dyoon

The Bracelet

In this poem Mira employs the imagery of an Indian wedding to express her one-pointed love for the Lord.

At the time of the wedding a bracelet, usually made of cardamom and nuts, is put on the bride's wrist. It can to some extent be compared to the wedding ring in the West, except that the bracelet is tied by the bride's parents or some elderly relative.

Mira, by putting on the bracelet of her Lord, has become His bride. She refuses to put on the bracelet of anybody else. In other words, engrossed in the thought of the Lord, she is now averse to paying attention to the world and its objects.

Describing the various steps of the wedding ceremony, Mira says that it was her Master who decorated her as the bride and effected the divine union. She ends the poem with a prayer to the Lord to grant her the shelter of her Master.

> I'll not don the bracelet, friend,
> Of other than my Husband.
> He who was the loved one of mine
> Has become my Groom Divine.
>
> My Master gave me to eat
> Of knowledge, the precious sweet,*
> And fondly then did he bedeck
> With love's divine garland my neck.†
> I'll not don the bracelet, friend,
> Of other than my Husband.

---

* After the bracelet is put around the bride's wrist, the parents give her a sweet or piece of candy to eat.
† Next, a garland of fresh flowers is put around her neck.

And what kept flitting, like the wind,
He made an awning* of that mind.

From my body He did design
An archway,† subtle and sublime.
He who was the loved one of mine
Is now my wedded Spouse Divine.

The Master then on my wrist did tie
The band‡ of Truth no gem could vie.
Now who can snap it off my hand?

I'll not don the bracelet, friend,
Of other than my Husband.

The wedding guests, pure and divine,
With pleasure came at the marriage time.
I thus attained the aim of life –
To be the Eternal One's wife.

He who was the loved one of mine
Is my wedded Groom Divine.

---

* A dignified and well-decorated awning is made, under which the father gives
away the bride.
† The forehead has been described by Indian, and also Persian, mystics as
an arch or archway, through which the soul has to pass in order to enter the
inner regions.
‡ *Kankan*, a specially designed coloured band that is tied around the wrist of
the bride at the time of the wedding.

Mira dons the bracelet in her hand,
A gift from her Eternal Husband.
O Lord, Thee do I humbly entreat,
Grant the shelter of my Master's feet.

I'll not don the bracelet, friend,
Of other than my Husband.

He who was the loved one of mine –
I'm wedded to that Groom Divine.

MSS, p.405
Naheen baandhoon meendhhal

Within Thy Body

In this small poem Mira points out the spiritual treasures that lie within the human body. The sweet strains of the divine melody reverberate within the body. Brilliant light, wondrous sights, and even the Lord Himself are within the human frame. This the Saints alone know, for they have free access to the eternal home of the Lord.

Within your body the gong resounds
In sweet strains of eternal song.
Within your body of ten doors,
Day and night rumbles the sound of the drum.

In your body are gardens with rare blooms,
But a honeybee alone will seek their fragrance.
Within your body burns a flame
In resounding waves of brilliant light.

The Lord's glory, O Mira,
The Saints alone do know;
To His eternal home
Freely they come and go.

MSS, p.750
Vaage chhe re vaage chhe taari kaaya maan

The Lord as the Guest

Expressing her deep love and longing for the Lord, Mira prays
to Him to come and meet her. Once He comes, she says, she will
hold Him like a rare jewel or lodge Him within the chamber of
her heart as a cherished guest.

> O my friend, dear Lord,
> My heart longs to meet Thee.
> Once Thou art in my sight,
> Never will I let Thee part;
> I'll firmly hold Thee close,
> As one clasps a rare jewel.

> Pray heed my prayer and come,
> Else Thy name 'Redeemer'
> Will be put to shame.
> When I think of Thee, come;
> In my heart's chamber
> I'll have Thee as my guest.

> Be merciful, O Lord,
> Grant me a glimpse of Thee.
> Only at Thy lotus feet
> Is my haven.

In the world's stormy ocean
I am tossing about;
Who else but Thee can hold
My hand and save me.

Says Mira, O Lord, have mercy;
There is none as gracious as Thee.

MSS, p.328
Olyoon thaari aave ho

The Anchorite

Mira rejects the ways of the ascetics of her time and lays stress on the importance of imbibing divine qualities within, instead of an outward show of piety.

This poem is presumably addressed to the anchorites of a particular school, who wear specially designed robes, dye their clothes in an ochre colour, pierce their ears in order to wear large earrings, carry a wooden vessel for water, hold in their hands a single-stringed instrument and go singing and begging from door to door.

Mira says that she will gladly become an anchorite, but with a difference. She will adorn herself with the robes that please her Master; in other words, she will adopt a way of life which her Master likes and approves. She will dye her garment in the hue of the true knowledge imparted by her Master, and make her body the lyre to produce esoteric tunes within. She will lovingly sing the song of the Lord's praises and cling to His feet in the inner regions. Mira concludes that becoming such an anchorite, she will always remain in the company of the Saints.

> Such an anchorite I'll become, O friend!
> Whatever attire would please my Master,
> With that I will gladly bedeck myself.
>
> With purity, contentment and poise,
> My body's vessel I'll eagerly fill;
> The One who is beyond illusion's pale,
> On Him alone will I now meditate.

In the hue of the knowledge my Master gave,
I'll dye my garment in a shade fast and deep,
And will pierce my mind
To wear submission's ring.

With love I will fondly sing the Lord's praises
And hold in a firm embrace His lotus feet;
I'll make a lyre of this body of mine,
And without a break repeat His Name.

O Lord of Mira, Thou Almighty One,
Thus would I abide in the Saint's company.

MSS, p.381
Baala main bairaagan hoongi

As You Deem Fit

Mira says that by herself she cannot cross the ocean of the world. She has nothing to do with yoga, oblation, penance and such practices. She only adores the Lord and longs for Him. She implores Him to ferry her across; but in a spirit of acceptance of the Lord's will, she asks Him to do so only if He deems fit.

Whenever you deem fit,
Ferry me across, my Lord.
My boat is frail and decrepit;
How can I reach the other shore?

The Vedas and all holy books
Have kept singing your praises,
But know not your true merit.
Neither yoga nor oblation,
Nor penance nor austerity
Do I know or indulge in.
Continually I devote myself
To Nam – the essence of all worship.

I have waited for long, waited
For you to come, O Saviour of all.
Beloved Lord of Mira!
I adore your lotus feet
And fondly take their refuge.

MSS, p.328
Man maane jab taar prabhuji

The Ways of the Swan

Mira has become one with her Master and whatever tales the people may tell about her, she is firm in her devotion. The worldly people cannot comprehend the ways of the devotees, just as a crow cannot gauge the qualities of a swan. Mira ends the song by stressing the importance of satsang, association with the Saints, in order to be rid of the bondage of birth and death in this world.

> Whatever the people may say,
> My heart now remains in the Lord.
>
> Mira has merged into the Saint,
> As does *suhaaga* blend with gold.
> Mira is one with her Master,
> As is a thread with the cloth.
>
> People say Mira has gone astray;
> They're prey, alas, to their own delusion.
> The gait of a swan, only the swan knows;
> What could the crow ever know
>   of the swan's ways?*

---

* It is believed that the swans love their abode in the divine lake, Mansarovar, live only on pearls and have the ability to separate milk from water. Saints often use the image of the swan for the spiritually evolved soul and the crow for the person deeply attached to the world and ignorant of the inner regions.

Mira lay asleep in the vale of darkness
Until her Master shook her from
    the slumber of eons.*

Having got the precious human form,
Who sings not the glory of the Lord
Will, indeed, be a morsel for Kal.†
O friend, keep the company of Saints;
Worship with love your almighty Lord.
Thus will your coming and going end.

By the grace of Mira's beloved Lord,
The chains of birth and death are broken.

MSS, p.848
Koi Kachhu kahe man laaga re

---

* In some versions of the poem, these two lines are slightly different. They read:
"My mind that was for eons lost in sleep, / Awoke on hearing the Master's
Word."
† The negative power.

The Lover's Prayer

This is another song of Mira set to a folk tune which, even now, is popular in Rajasthan. The refrain is followed by couplets known as *dohas*,* which may or may not be thematically connected. Thus the song deals with love, the difference between worldly and spiritual love, advice to a devotee or lover, and it ends on the happy note of meeting the Master.

> Thee alone, O Lord, do I adore.
> Break not the bond of love, I pray;
> Let my love grow from day to day.
> Love me, oh love me, more and more;
> Thee alone, O Lord, do I adore.
>
> Earlier, had I come to know
> That the path of love is that of woe,
> I would have called to the beat of a drum:
> None, oh none, in love's lane should come.
>
> Break not the bond of love, I pray;
> Let my love grow from day to day.
> Love me, oh love me, more and more;
> Thee alone, O Lord, do I adore.

---

*The *doha*, also known as a *sakhi*, is a two-line composition. Each line is divided in two parts; thus the couplets here have been rendered in four lines. *Dohas* are mostly sung to a different tune from the melody of the refrain.

Boiling milk never try to drink;
From the friendship of fools* ever shrink –
One moment warm, next cold as ice,
Friend in a flash, foe in a trice.

Break not the bond of love, I pray;
Let my love grow from day to day.

Who takes to love is mad, no doubt;
Firm in love as a pillar stout
Is a true lover, rare and cool;
Who breaks his love – a heartless fool.

Love me, oh love me, more and more;
Thee alone, O Lord, do I adore.

Strong as a crystal rock Thou art;
A wall of sand, I'm faint of heart.
How to love Thee? O Lord of mine;
O precious Lord, pray make me Thine.

Break not the bond of love, I pray;
Oh let it grow from day to day.
Love me, oh love me, more and more;
Thee alone, O Lord, do I adore.

---

* By the term 'fool' Mira implies worldly people, whose association is not lasting.

Swollen in the rains, rushing high,
But soon to ebb and become dry;
Deceptive like that mountain brook,
Deep and flowing world's love may look.

Break not the bond of love, I pray;
Let my love grow from day to day.

'Tis monsoon, full of bliss and trance;
In joy and glee the peacocks dance.
My Master now with me does stay;
The wind my woe has blown away.

Break not the bond of love, I pray;
Let my love grow from day to day.
Love me, oh love me, more and more;
Thee, O Lord, does Mira adore.

MSS, p.444
Ramaiya mere ab tohi soon laago neh

The Bond of Ego

In this song Mira, having met the Lord, expresses her feelings of joy and ecstasy. But, she points out, it was only after she became free from the bonds of ego and the guiles of mind that the veil from the inner eye was removed and she could obtain her object.

> I am steeped in the love of the Lord,
> And I am rid of the guiles of my mind.
>
> As long as I was a captive of ego and pride,
> My Beloved never cast a glance at me.
> But when this slave became humble as the dust,
> From my eye He removed the inner veil.
>
> He has bridged the gap of separation;
> Now He has embraced me and made me His own.
> I drink deep from the goblet of His love,
> And now live with my Beloved ever in bliss.
>
> Family pride and fear of the world's opinion –
> These ties I have cut as one breaks a thread.
> The Lord has become one with His devotee,
> As *suhaaga* merges into gold.
>
> My mind now recoils from all that is false;
> My Lord is ever pleased with those who are true.
> Fortunate, indeed, is Mira,
> That the Lord has become her own.

MSS, p.380
Raam rang laago, mere dil ko dhoko bhaago

Tidings of the Beloved

This song of Mira is based on the imagery of a lonely wife whose husband has gone to a distant land. She is unable to go and meet him, as the way is arduous, beset with unscalable mountains, deep ravines and dense forests. She longs to hear news of her husband and inquires about his welfare from the wayfarers who happen to pass by her village.

Here Mira, in the same vein, longs to obtain tidings of her Beloved, whose abode is far beyond the ocean of the world. Like the loving and faithful wife, she remembers the virtues of her Beloved and her thoughts are always on His lotus feet.

> From whom shall I inquire, O friend,
> From whom will I ever obtain
> The tidings of my beloved Lord?
>
> Distant is my Dear One's abode;
> The way is beset with hills steep,
> With ravines deep and forests dense;
> And beyond, across the ocean, lives my Husband.
>
> When the string of a necklace breaks,
> The pearls scatter all about; likewise,
> Breaking the bounds of my endurance,
> Tears flow freely and drench my dress.

I try to sleep, but sleep from my eyes has fled;
The misery of my waking moments
Is too intense for words to convey.
Says Mira, O beloved Lord,
I think only of Thy virtues
And in Thy feet remain absorbed.

MSS, p.207
Kene poochaan kene re poochaan

Let Not the Lord Go

This short poem is brimming with Mira's love for the Lord. She does not want to let Him out of her sight even for a moment. To keep looking at Him, to please Him and to enshrine Him within her heart is all she wants.

Oh, do not let such a beloved Lord go.
To Him sacrifice your body, wealth and mind;
Enshrine Him within the depths of your heart.

Come, my friends, let us behold His lovely face
And drink with our eyes the nectar of His charm.

Whatever ways are pleasing to the Beloved,
With them let us lovingly adorn ourselves.

His visage is beautiful, soothing to the eyes;
Let looking at His face be our very life.

It is only the rare and fortunate ones
Who please Mira's beloved Lord.

MSS, p.469
Aise prabhu jaan na deejai ho

The Way of the Tree

The devotee should be compassionate, benevolent and tolerant in his dealings. He should face the ups and downs of life with detachment and courage. In his pursuit of true knowledge, he should be steadfast and firm. Mira uses the example of a fruit-bearing tree to emphasize this point.

> O mind, adopt the ways of the tree
> And from the cares of the world become free.
>
> Those who come to cut it, it does not hate,
> Nor adores them who come to irrigate.
> Even to those who hurl stones with force
> It yields fruits, with no touch of remorse.
>
> Gales and storms and the fury of rain –
> It suffers all, yet does not complain.
> It bears winter's frost and summer's heat
> To provide wayward birds a snug retreat.
>
> Likewise attain an unconcerned state,
> And on the Lord lovingly meditate.
> If for redemption you truly pine,
> Repeat continually His Name Divine.
> As a *chaatrik's** thoughts are in the rain,
> Let His feet in your heart remain.
> Thus you will devotion's nectar find
> And meet Mira's Lord, merciful and kind.

MSS, p.768
Mana to vrikshan ki lat le'i

---

*The rainbird: in Indian folklore the rainbird is always longing for the rain.

While There Is Sunshine

This is one of the few poems of Mira which sound a note of warning. A person remains engaged in worldly pursuits all his life. He never tries to take advantage of the rare privilege of human birth by turning towards God. However, at the time of death he hopes to attain salvation by trying to remember the Lord. He had the chance to find the path of devotion, but he wasted his life in vain pursuits. At the moment of death he drinks water made 'holy' by the touch of *tulsi** leaves, puts the sacred mark of *tilak*[†] on his forehead, asks his relations to repeat aloud God's names—all in the hope of salvation. Mira says that all this is nothing but self-deception. An ignorant fool will not become a learned scholar after death, nor a robber turn into a holy man. Through a few simple examples, Mira points out that efforts at self-improvement and God realization have to be made while there is still time, while the sun still shines.

> All your life, never did you love the Lord;
> On the verge of death you expect to become a saint!
>
> When your house is ablaze you rush to dig a well;
> How can you then quench the flames?
> When thieves have robbed you of all your wealth,
> Of what use is your lighting the lamp?

---

*In orthodox Hindu families a few drops of water infused with the leaves of the basil plant (*tulsi*) used to be given to the dying person at the time of death. It was believed that the departing soul would thereby attain liberation.

[†] A mark made on the forehead mostly out of vermilion paste or sandalwood paste. In earlier times it was believed that such a mark made on the forehead of the dying person would lead to his salvation.

You spent your childhood in mirth and play;
Youth you wasted in the pursuit of pleasures,
And clung to children in your old age.
Now at death's approach you ask for salvation!

When the lake was dry you did not raise a dike;
Now that all the water has streamed away,
What use are your efforts to build a dam?
You knew the right course, but never did act;
Now at the hour of your impending death
You get *tulsi* leaves and put *tilak* on your forehead,
And ask kinfolk to recite God's name to you.

Says Mira, O ignorant and foolish one,
You are deceiving your own self and none else.

MSS, p.780
Paheli prabhu shoon preet na baandhi

The Craving of Mira's Eyes

Once having enjoyed the bliss of a glimpse of the Beloved, Mira's eyes have acquired the habit of constantly looking for Him. She 'sold' her entire being to the Lord the day she saw Him, and now awaits Him only.

Since the day my Beloved gave
His darshan, my eyes ever crave
A glimpse of His face, once again.
It's now their wont to look for Him;
They look for Him, they burn in pain.

His image, after luring my heart,
Keeps rankling like a pointed dart.
Without seeing Him I will for sure
Lose my life. Only the healing herb
Of His look can my suffering cure.

Long I've stood at the palace gate;
With eyes on the path, for Him I wait.
Her very self to the Lord has Mira sold,
To ever remain in His loving fold;
But 'She's gone astray,' people rave.
Since the day my Lord His darshan gave,
For a glimpse of Him my eyes still crave.

MBP, p.127
Nainaan more baan parri

The True Queen

When a devotee is absorbed in the ecstasy of inner spiritual bliss, the world starts looking upon her as mad. Such is Mira's own state. The sound of the drum is reverberating within the temple of her body. The swan, that is, the soul, has vacated the body, and now to Mira her body appears alien. Having reached the radiant feet of the Master within, she has now truly become a queen.

> Mira's gone mad, helpless is she;
> Beyond all help is her malady.

> In her temple within, the drum she beats;
> To the sound of the drum she repeats
> The Lord's Name in sweet melody.
> The vessel has broken, the water
> Is spilled; away flies the swan.
> Mira's body is alien –
> A stranger to her.

> Mira's gone mad, helpless is she;
> Beyond all help is her malady.

> In the streets and the squares
> Mira firmly declares:
> At her Master's feet
> She'll forever stay.
> Now she's truly a queen
> And supreme is her sway.

Mira's gone mad, helpless is she;
Beyond all cure is her malady.

MSS, p.847
Meera ho ga'i divaani

A Rainy Day

In this simple poem Mira, expressing her joy on meeting her beloved Lord, conveys her emotions more through subtle suggestion than direct affirmation.

Just as the lakes and ponds, after remaining dry due to a long spell of drought, have become happily full with the onset of the rains, Mira, distraught and pining in separation, is full of bliss with the arrival of her Beloved. Now that He has come home to her, Mira wishes the rain to continue to pour so that He may be unable to leave her.

> It's raining today, let it pour;
> My love is home, Him I adore.
>
> Dense clouds in the sky now hover;
> In tender drops do they shower.
> Lakes and ponds that were dry and drained,
> Becoming full have their joy regained.
>
> It's raining today, let it pour;
> My love is home, Him I adore.
>
> For Him many days did I pine;
> I've met Him, and now He is mine.
> I am with Thee, pray do not part;
> Fear of parting pulls at my heart.
>
> It's raining today, let it pour;
> My love is home, Him I adore.

Deep is Mira's love, now free from pain;
Her Primal Groom is with her again.
It's raining today, let it pour;
My love is home, Him I adore.

MSS, p.441
Meha barasavo kare re

The Beloved Comes Home

Intense longing to meet the Beloved develops and strengthens love, and invariably leads to union with Him. This song of union conveys the bliss of Mira who, after having suffered untold agony in separation, has reached the presence of her Beloved. She expresses her feelings with a tender yet vibrant joy.

O friends, the Beloved has come home.
He whom this separated one awaited,
Whom day after day she longed to meet,
That same loved one, O friend, has come.

The world's rarest jewels
I'll lay at His feet;
I'll adore Him, adore Him
With all my heart and soul.
I will even cherish the one
Who first brought the news of His coming.

My five friends have come together
To sing auspicious songs of joy;
They rejoice with me
For my bliss of union –
Bliss that I cannot contain
Within the depths of my heart.

I have become attached to Him,
The ocean of tenderness;
My eyes remain spellbound
By the charm of His love,
And the courtyard of Mira's heart
Is drenched with the shower of bliss.

MSS, p.512
Saheliaan saajan ghar aaya ho

One with the Ocean

When the devotee's inner eye opens, he comes in contact with the Radiant Form of his Master, the beauty and brilliance of which is both magnetic and enchanting. When the coverings of matter, mind and maya are removed, the devotee's soul, shining in its pristine purity, becomes one with the inner Radiant Form. The bonds that had kept the soul tied to the physical, astral and causal worlds are finally broken; and the soul is engulfed in divine love or 'His love's snare', as Mira puts it. The lover has now become one with the Beloved. The drop, having merged in the ocean, has become the ocean.

> I raised my eyes for just one look
> At Him, the bewitcher of all.
> His radiant beauty pierced my being;
> It lingers still within my heart.
>
> The moment I lifted
> The veil from my face,
> My tiny spark merged
> In the divine flame.
> What use in repenting,
> What avail brooding now,
> When I have been caught
> In His love's snare?
>
> Mira's Beloved is almighty;
> The drop is now one
> With love's great ocean.

MSS, p.513
Aa'i dekhan manmohan koon

ENDNOTES

1. *Mira Sudha Sindhu*, p.779:87 (hereafter referred to as *MSS*).
2. *MSS*, p.384:18.
3. *MSS*, p.196:102.
4. *MSS*, p.753–4:16.
5. *Mira Brihat Padavali*, Part I, p.201:423 (hereafter referred to as *MBP*).
6. *MSS*, p.281:35.
7. *MBP*, p.207:431.
8. *Mirabai ki Shabdavali*, p.31.
9. *MSS*, p.377:1.
10. *MSS*, p.479:28.
11. *MSS*, p.281:34.
12. *MSS*, p.292:66.
13. *MSS*, p.295:72 (lines 1, 4, 5).
14. *MSS*, p.265:1.
15. *Mirabai ka Jiwan-vritta evam Kavya*, p.120:156.
16. *MSS*, p.847, (lines 3, 6).
17. *MSS*, p.483:41.
18. *MBP*, p.247:505.
19. *Mirabai ka Jiwan-vritta evam Kavya*, p.129:192 (lines 4, 5).
20. *MSS*, p.279:29.
21. *MSS*, p.279:29.
22. Given in "Chaurasi Vaishnavon ki Varta", a manuscript written in 1640.
23. *MSS*, p.768:54.
24. *MSS*, p.760:31.
25. *Mirabai ka Jiwan-vritta evam Kavya*, p.53.
26. Goetz, *Mira Bai*, p.40.
27. *MSS*, p.753:14.
28. *MSS*, p.281:34 (lines 6, 7).
29. *MSS*, p.407:82 (lines 4, 6, 7).

30. *MSS*, p.846:15.
31. *MSS*, p.280:32 (lines 4, 6).
32. *MSS*, p.402:68.
33. *MSS*, p.523:44 (lines 1–3).
34. *Adi Granth*, Suhi, M3:754.
35. *MSS*, p.759:29 [G.].
36. *MBP*, p.139:292 (lines 1, 2, 9, 10).
37. *MBP*, p.239:493 (lines 1, 2, 8, 9).
38. *Mirabai ki Shabdavali*, p.24:63.
39. *MSS*, p.842:5 (line 3).
40. *Mirabai ki Shabdavali*, p.9.
41. *Mirabai ka Jiwan-vritta evam Kavya*, p.131:201 (lines 3, 4).
42. *MSS*, p.399:55 (line 6).
43. *MSS*, p.750:7 [G.].
44. *MSS*, p.875:20.
45. *MSS*, p.196:102 (lines 1, 3).
46. *MBP*, p.246:504 (lines 1–4).
47. *MSS*, p.748:4.
48. *MBP*, p.271.
49. *MSS*, p.841:2 (line 3).
50. *MSS*, p.167:22 (lines 6, 7).
51. *MSS*, p.750:8.
52. *MSS*, p.767:52 (lines 1–3, 11, 12).
53. *MSS*, p.759:30 (lines 1, 4, 6) [G.].
54. *MSS*, p.772:66 (lines 1, 5). [G].
55. *MSS*, p.386:24 (lines 6, 7).
56. *MSS*, p.755:22 (lines 2–5).
57. *MSS*, p.767–8:52 (lines 5–10, 12).
58. *MBP*, p.161:341 (line 1).
59. *MSS*, p.380:10 (lines 8, 9).
60. *MSS*, p.441:1.
61. *MSS*, p.515:21 (lines 1–4). [G].
62. *MBP*, p.127:264.
63. *Mira, Vyaktitwa aur Kartritwa*, p.271.
64. *MSS*, p.444:12 (lines 3, 4).
65. *MSS*, p.379:9 (lines 2, 10).
66. *MSS*, p.928:15.

GLOSSARY

Adi Granth   Primal (*aadi*) book or scripture (*granth*); also called the
Granth Sahib; the name given to the scripture that brings together
the poetry of the first five Gurus and the ninth Guru in the line
of Guru Nanak, as well as numerous Saints from various parts of
India and neighbouring countries. The Adi Granth, one of India's
most sacred scriptures, is a mosaic of esoteric poetry by Saints
from various religious, cultural, vocational and geographic back-
grounds whose teachings emphasize the oneness of God, the path
of the Word, the equality of all people and the pursuit of truth.

Amardas, Guru (1479–1574)   The third successor in the line of
Guru Nanak, Guru Amar Das, from Punjab, came to his master,
Guru Angad, late in life at the age of sixty-one. He is credited with
starting the institution of the *langar* (free community kitchen).
His extensive writings are included in the Adi Granth.

brahmins   The priestly class; the first and the highest of the four
castes into which Hindu society was divided. The role of the
brahmins includes the acquisition and imparting of the knowledge contained in the Vedas and other religious literature,
assistance in or the actual performance of rites and rituals, and
the bestowal and receipt of charity.

darshan   Beholding, seeing, viewing, looking at someone with
admiration, love and reverence. Outer darshan is looking at one's
Master, or an image of a deity, with such absorption that one
forgets everything else and loses the sense of separate existence.
The darshan that the mystics generally talk about, however, and
the one that elevates the soul to spheres of higher consciousness

is inner darshan, the darshan of the Radiant Form of the Master or the lord of a high inner region.

Dwarka   An ancient city situated on the coast of western India; regarded by Hindus as one of the holiest of their pilgrimage sites.

eighty-four   The 'wheel of eighty-four', the wheel of transmigration. The name indicates the eight million four hundred thousand life forms into which a soul may have to incarnate.

feet of the Master   *See* lotus feet.

jogi   A variant of 'yogi'. *See* yogi.

Kabir (1398–1518)   Born in Varanasi (formerly Kashi or Banaras), Kabir Sahib travelled throughout India, teaching the practice of the Word. He earned a meagre living as a weaver and, as a result of his outspoken condemnation of ritualistic observances, faced unrelenting opposition from the priestly class. Some of his writings were incorporated into the Adi Granth. His writings are still widely quoted in daily life throughout India and have become part of folk music and culture.

Kal   Time or death; the ruler of the three worlds who administers justice strictly according to the law of karma. Dependent for all power on the Supreme Being, Kal is the universal mind, known also as Yama (the god of death), Brahm or Dharmrai. The domain of Kal is the whole creation up to Trikuti, which includes the physical, astral and causal worlds. Kal is the personification of the negative force in the creation, in contradistinction to Dayal (the Merciful), the eternal positive power, the Supreme Being.

karma   Action and reaction; the law of cause and effect; the fruits or results of past thoughts, words and deeds. Under this law, the soul has to face the consequences of all its actions. It is the law of karma that keeps the soul imprisoned in the creation, as it has to keep taking birth after birth to account for its actions in previous lives.

Krishna   One of the most widely revered of the Hindu gods; an incarnation of Vishnu (the preserver god in the Hindu trinity) and the subject of many devotional works. The Bhagavad Gita, one of the most popular books on Hindu philosophy, embodies his expositions on the paths of selfless action, knowledge, devotion and meditation.

lotus feet The lotus flower is associated with purity, delicacy and beauty; although it grows in mud and water, it remains untouched by them. Out of reverence, the feet of the Master, of a holy man or of a deity are referred to as lotus feet. At the time of initiation, the Master places his Shabd form, called the Radiant Form, in the spiritual heart of the disciple. In the course of the disciple's inner evolution, when this form manifests itself within, it is the Master's feet that first appear at the eight-petalled lotus, a microcosmic centre on the astral plane—hence the expression 'lotus feet'. This is the point of contact between the soul and the Shabd and the beginning of the soul's journey into higher regions.

Maya Illusion, delusion, unreality; the phenomenal universe. Maya denotes everything that comes and goes, that is transient. The entire creation (the physical, astral and causal worlds) is described as illusory or false because it is impermanent, in contrast to Satnam (the true Name), the Supreme Being, which alone is permanent, eternal and true. Maya is often described as the web of illusion and is sometimes personified as a goddess.

Nam In Sant Mat terminology, Nam (*naam*, the Name) represents not only the dynamic power of God that created and sustains the universe, but also the current that can unite souls with God. In order to elevate human consciousness, which normally operates at the gross level of mind and senses, Nam functions at two levels: at the human level as the initiation mantra granted by a true Master and at God's level as the divine melody called Shabd, experienced through soul consciousness. *See also* Shabd.

nirat The faculty of the soul to see within. Unless nirat is sufficiently developed, proper *dhyan* (inner contemplation) is not possible. *See also* surat.

Paltu (1710–1780)   Born in Nanga-Jalalpur in Uttar Pradesh, Paltu Sahib lived in Ayodhya, a town sacred to the Hindus, where he was a grocer by profession. A disciple and successor of Gobind Sahib, Paltu fearlessly denounced the rituals and customs of organized religion. For his bold utterances he was persecuted and burnt alive by the enraged orthodoxy. His poems, which convey his message directly to the hearts of his readers, are published under the title *Paltu Sahib ki Bani*.

prakritis   Nature; the essential nature of mind and matter which projects itself in various forms of emotions and actions and which also influences the various parts of the body. According to Hindu philosophy, there are twenty-five prakritis that consist of the five principal manifestations of the five elements or tattwas that make up the human body.

Radiant Form   Light form; astral form. At the time of initiation the Master projects his Radiant Form within the disciple from Shabd, which is the real and ultimate form of the Master. The Radiant Form is also called the Shabd form of the Master. *See also* lotus feet.

Ravidas (c.1414–1540)   Born in Varanasi (formerly Banaras), Ravidas is also known as Guru Ravidas, Raidas, Ruidas or Rohidas. He was a disciple of Ramanand and earning his living as a cobbler, travelled widely, teaching the path of devotion to the Word. His initiates included Pipa, a Rajput king of Gagaraungarh, as well as Mira Bai, princess of Mewar. The Adi Granth includes some of his poems.

Sant Mat   The teachings or path (*mat*) of the Saints (*sant*). The term was popularized by the eighteenth-century Saint Tulsi Sahib of Hathras and was adopted by Soami Ji of Agra. It refers to the teachings common to true Saints: the science of merging one's soul with the supreme Creator through contact with the Word (Shabd).

Satguru   True (*sat*) spiritual teacher (*guru*); a Master who has access to Sach Khand, the fifth inner region. In Sant Mat terminology, a Satguru is a Saint who is ordained to take certain allotted souls back to God by initiating them into Surat Shabd Yoga.

Sat Lok   True (*sat*) region (*lok*). The entire universe is described either in terms of five regions above the physical plane or four planes of existence—the physical, astral, causal-spiritual and pure spiritual (Pind, And, Brahmand and Sat Lok). The plane of Sat Lok is further divided into four stages: Sach Khand, Alakh, Agam and Anami (Radha Soami). Saints have sometimes used Sat Lok and Sach Khand as synonyms.

Shabd   Sound, voice, word, hymn; esoterically, the underlying current of divine energy that created and sustains the universe; also called Word, Name, Holy Spirit, sound current, unstruck music, the music of the spheres and so forth. It was through Shabd, the eternal power of God, that souls were sent down from their original home to inhabit the creation, and it is through the same power that they must retrace their journey homewards. However, no one but a living true Master can reveal the secret of Shabd and connect the disciple's consciousness to it. A shabd is also a song, a hymn, a religious or spiritual poem.

simran   Remembrance, recollection, repetition of holy names; calling to mind or meditating upon the Supreme Being. It is through simran, the first part of the spiritual practice as taught by the Saints, that the attention is withdrawn from the outer world and concentrated at the eye centre.

suhaaga   Borax or the salt of boron. It is used for purifying gold and for bringing out its lustre. In folklore it is believed that borax in the process becomes one with gold.

surat   Soul, soul consciousness, the attention of the soul. Surat refers to the ability of the soul to concentrate within and experience the bliss of inner regions; it refers particularly to the faculty of the soul to hear the divine Sound or Shabd within, whereas nirat refers to the faculty of the soul to see within. When the soul travels within, it hears the melody of Shabd through surat.

Tukaram (1598–1650)   Reared in a well-to-do family of traders in Dehu in the District of Pune, Tukaram was blessed with initiation by Babaji Raghava Chaitanya in 1619. He subsequently lost interest in the family business and became a mystic adept. During the remainder of his life he composed thousands of poems denouncing all outward forms of worship. His poems, which remain popular even today, are published under the titles *Saarth Shri Tukaramachi Gatha* and *Shri Tukaram Bavanchya Abhanganchi Gatha*.

Vedas   Literally, knowledge; revealed knowledge as embodied in the four ancient Hindu scriptures (Rig Veda, Sama Veda, Yajur Veda, Atharva Veda); also refers to Vedic literature in general, including the Upanishads and various interpretive texts. The Vedas deal with spiritual matters, the divine powers of gods, sacred formulas (mantras) and the problems of life in the world. The Vedas reveal that some of their authors knew about the Word of God, which they called *naad* (Sound) or *vaak* (Word).

yogi   A practitioner of yoga, a system of physical, mental or spiritual exercise, especially one that aims at union of the soul with God.

Bibliography

Hindi

Barathwal, Pitambardutta. *Hindi Kavya Mein Nirgun Sampradaya*. Publication information not available.

Behari, Bankey. *Braj-Chandra-Chakori Mira*. Vrindavan: Shri Radhika Pustakalya Tatha Prakashan Trust, 1951.

Chaturvedi, Parashuram. *Uttari Bharat ki Sant Parampara*. 2nd ed. Allahabad: Bharati Bhandar, 1964 [2021 Vikrami].

Das, Brajratan. *Mira Madhuri*. 2nd ed. Varanasi: Hindi Sahitya Kutir, 1956 [2013 Vikrami].

Gehlot, Mahavirsingh. *Mira: Jivan aur Kavya*. Publication information not available.

Hari, Viyogi. *Mira*. Publication information not available.

———. *Daya*. Publication information not available.

———. *Sahjobai*. Publication information not available.

Hindi Vishva-Kosh. Vol. 1. Edited by Nagendra Nath Basu. Reprint (original Calcutta: 1928). Delhi: B.R. Publishing Corp., 1986.

Lal, Shrikrishna. *Mirabai: Jivancharitra aur Alochana*. Publication information not available.

'Madhav', Bhuveneshwarnath Mishra. *Mira ki Prem Sadhana*. 4th ed. Delhi: Raj Kamal Prakashan, n.d.

Mirabai. *Mirabai ki Padavali*. Edited by Parashuram Chaturvedi. 3rd ed. Prayag: Hindi Sahitya Sammelan, 1947 [2004 Vikrami].

———. *Mirabai ki Shabdavali*. 8th ed. Allahabad: Belvedere Printing Works, 1973.

————. *Mira Brihat Padavali.* 2 vols. Edited by Shri Harnarianji Purohit. Jodhpur: Rajasthan Oriental Research Institute, 1968/75.

Nabhadas. *Bhaktamal.* Commentary by Priyadas and Roopkala. Lucknow: Tej Kumar Press, 1964.

Nath, Gokul. *Chaurasi Vaishnava ki Varta.* Publication information not available.

Ojha, Gourishankar Hirashankar. *Rajputane ka Itihas.* Publication information not available.

————. *Udaipur Rajya ka Itihas.* Publication information not available.

Prabhat, C.L. *Mirabai.* Bombay: Hindi Granth Ratnakar, 1965.

Priyadas. *Bhaktiras Bodhini (Tika).* Lucknow: Naval Kishore Press, 1926.

Sarin, Dharampal. *Neech se Oonch Kiyo Mere Satguru.* New Delhi: S. Chand, n.d.

Shabnam, Padmavati. *Mira, Vyaktitwa aur Kartritwa.* Varanasi: Hindi Pracharak Sansthan, 1973.

Sharma, B.P. *Sant Guru Ravidas.* Chandigarh: Guru Ravidas Sansthan, n.d.

Sharma, Krishnadev. *Mirabai-Padavali.* Delhi: Regal Book Depot, 1973.

Shekhawat, Kalyansingh. *Mirabai ka Jiwan-vritta evam Kavya.* Ratanada Jodhpur: Hindi Sahitya Mandir, 1974.

Singh, Moti. *Nirgun Sahitya: Sanskritik Prishtabhumi.* Varanasi: Nagri Pracharni Sabha, 1962.

Singh, Rajdev. *Hindi ki Nirgun Kavyadhara aur Kabir.* Delhi: Alekh Prakashan, 1981.

Srivastava, Murlidhar. *Mira Darshan.* 2nd ed. Allahabad: Sahitya Bhawan, 1964.

————. *Mira ki Bhakti aur Unki Kavya Sadhana ka Anusheelan.* Allahabad: Sahitya Bhawan, 1974.

Swaroop, Anand Swami. *Mira Sudha Sindhu.* Bhilwara: Shri Mira Prakashan Samiti, 1957 [2014 Vikrami].

Tiwari, Bhagwandas. *Mira ki Pramanik Padavali.* Allahabad: Sahitya Bhawan, 1974.

Trigunayat, Govind. *Kabir ki Vichardhara.* Kanpur: Sahitya Niketan, 1952.

Tripathi, Ramnaresh. *Kavita Kaumudi.* Pt. 1. Publication information not available.

Yogendra Singh. *Sant Raidas.* Delhi: Akshar Prakashan, 1972.

Marathi
Mahipati. *Bhaktivijay.* Publication information not available.

Tukaram. *Shri Tukarambavanchya Abbanganchi Gatha.* Edited by P.M. Lad. Punei: Maharashtra Government, 1991.

Punjabi
Adi Granth. *Shabdarth Sri Guru Granth Sahib.* 4 vols. Amritsar: Shiromani Gurdwara Prabandhak, 1999.

Nabha, Bhai Kahan Singh. *Mahan Kosha.* Delhi: National Book Shop, 1998.

English
Behari, Bankey. *Bhakta Mira.* Bombay: Bharatiya Vidya Bhavan, 1961.

Dhingra, Baldoon. *Songs of Meera: Lyrics in Ecstasy.* Orient Paperbacks, 1977.

Farquhar, J.N. *An Outline of Religious Literature in India.* London: Oxford University Press, 1920.

Goetz, Hermann. *Mira Bai, Her Life and Times.* Bombay: Bharatiya Vidya Bhawan, 1966.

Macauliffe, M.A. *The Sikh Religion.* Vol. 6. London: Oxford University Press, 1909.

Mehta, S.S. *Mirabai, the Saint of Mewad.* Bombay: Luza & Co., 1922.

Nilsson, Usha. *Mira Bai.* Sahitya Akademi, 1969.

Ranade, Ramchandra Dattatraya. *Pathway to God in Hindi Literature.* Bombay: Bharatiya Vidya Bhavan, 1959.

Sarda, Har Bilas. *Maharana Sanga: the Hindupat, the Last Great Leader of the Rajput Race.* Ajmer: Scottish Mission Industries, 1918.

Sen, Kshitimohan. *Medieval Mysticism of India*. Reprint (original 1935), New Delhi: Oriental Books Reprint Corp., 1974.

Tandon, R.C. *Songs of Mirabai*. Allahabad: Hindi Mandir, 1934.

Tod, James. *Annals and Antiquities of Rajasthan*. New Delhi: N.B.D. Publishers, 1978.

Varma, Ramkumar. *Kabir: Biography and Philosophy*. New Delhi: C.L. Gupta, 1977.

Vaswani, T.L. *Saint Mira*. Poona: Saint Mira's English Medium School, n.d.

INDEX OF HINDI/GUJARATI FIRST LINES

[G] indicates poems composed in the Gujarati language; all others are in Hindi.

215

Subject Index

anguish. *See* separation
attachment
  chains of, 98
  of the mind, 42
  to Master, 50, 175
  to Nam, 123
  to the Lord within, 116–17, 163
bliss, 16, 34, 35, 75, 88, 187, 195, 197
  of inner regions, 45, 92
  of union, 155, 200
body, home of the Lord, 35
company of saints, 164, 166.
  See also satsang
condemnation of external
  observances, 94, 179.
  See also rituals
cycle of birth and death. *See* death
darshan, 50, 58, 78, 83, 161, 190, 194
  bliss of, 75, 107, 194
  longing for, 48, 71–73.
  See also longing
death
  beyond cycle of birth and, 144
  cycle of birth and, 33, 55.
  See also transmigration
  of Mira. *See* Mira
desire for union, 116
desires, 42, 60. *See also* passions

detachment, 17, 74, 76, 81, 116,
  118, 123. *See also* attachment
  from slander, 108, 165
  from worldly bonds, 86, 109
  from worldly objects, 34
  through Nam, 131
  through Shabd, 156
devotion
  difficulties of, 61, 87, 88, 90, 164
  growth in, 90
  impact of Mira's, 22
  steadfastness in, 14, 76, 78, 80,
  91, 103, 108, 135, 158, 159, 163,
  164–65
disciple
  forbearance of, 21, 87
  helplessness of, 70, 113, 157, 195
  madness of, 88–89
  qualities of, 76, 191
  resolve of, 74
  restlessness of, 62, 64
  spiritual progress of, 106
  steadfastness of, 191
divine knowledge, 46, 107, 118, 120,
  125, 129, 149, 173, 179
divine love. *See* love
Divine Melody. *See* Shabd
ego, 134, 166

Addresses for Information and Books

INDIAN SUB-CONTINENT

INDIA
The Secretary
Radha Soami Satsang Beas
Dera Baba Jaimal Singh
District Amritsar, Punjab 143204

NEPAL
Mr. Dal Bahadur Shreshta
Radha Soami Satsang Beas
P. O. Box 1646
Gongabu, Dhapasi
Kathmandu
☎+97-1-435-7765

PAKISTAN
Mr. Sadrang Seetal Das
Lahori Mohala, Larkana
Sindh

SRI LANKA
Mr. Chandroo Mirpuri
39/3 Horton Place, Colombo 7

SOUTHEAST ASIA

FOR FAR EAST
Mrs. Cami Moss
RSSB-HK, T.S.T.,
P.O. Box 90745
Kowloon, Hong Kong
☎+852-2369-0625

MALAYSIA
Mr. Selvarajoo Pragasam
No. 15 Jalan SL 10/4
Bandar Sungai Long, Selangor
43000 Kajang

THAILAND
Mr. Harmahinder Singh Sethi
Radha Soami Satsang Beas
58/32 Rachdapitsek Road, Soi 16
Thapra, Bangkok Yai, Bangkok 10600
☎+66-2-868-2186 / 2187

INDONESIA
Mr. Ramesh Sadarangani
Jalan Pasir Putih IV/16, Block E 4
Ancol Timur, Jakarta
DKI Jakarta 14430

PHILIPPINES
Mr. Kay Sham
Science of the Soul Study Centre
9001 Don Jesus Boulevard
Alabang Hills, Cupang
Muntinlupa City, 1771
☎+63-2-772-0111 / 0555

SINGAPORE
Mrs. Asha Melwani
Radha Soami Satsang Beas
19 Amber Road, Singapore 439868
☎+65-6447-4956

ASIA PACIFIC

AUSTRALIA
Mr. Pradeep Raniga
P.O. Box 642
Balwyn North, Victoria 3104

NEW ZEALAND
Mr. Tony Waddicor
Science of the Soul Study Centre
P. O. Box 5331, Auckland
☎+64-9-624-2202

GUAM
Mrs. Hoori M. Sadhwani
115 Alupang Cove
241 Condo Lane, Tamuning 96911

HONG KONG
Mr. Manoj Sabnani
Radha Soami Satsang Beas
3rd Floor, Eader Centre
39-41 Hankow Road
Tsimshatsui, Kowloon
☎+852-2369-0625

JAPAN
Mr. Jani G. Mohinani
Radha Soami Satsang Beas
1-2-18 Nakajima-Dori
Aotani, Chuo-Ku, Kobe 651-0052
☎+81-78-222-5353

TAIWAN, R.O.C.
Mr. Haresh Buxani
Science of the Soul Study Group
Aetna Tower Office, 15F., No. 27-9
Sec.2, Jhongjheng E.Rd.
Danshuei Township, Taipei 25170
☎+886-2-8809-5223

NORTH AMERICA

CANADA
Mr. John Abel
#701-1012 Beach Avenue
Vancouver, B.C. V6E 1T7

Science of the Soul Study Centre
2934 -176th Street
Surrey, B.C. V3S 9V4
☎+1-604-541-4792

Mrs. Meena Khanna
149 Elton Park Road
Oakville, Ontario L6J 4C2

MEXICO
Mr. Jorge Villaseñor
Av. De Las Amapolas #39
Condominio Rancho Contento
Zapopan, Jalisco, C.P. 45010

UNITED STATES
Mr. Hank Muller
20038 Indigo Lake Drive
Magnolia, TX 77355

Dr. Vincent P. Savarese
2550 Pequeno Circle
Palm Springs
CA 92264-9522

Dr. Frank E. Vogel
275 Cutts Road
Newport, NH 03773

Dr. Douglas Torr
P.O. Box 2360, Southern Pines
NC 28388-2360

Science of the Soul Study Centre
4115 Gillespie Street
Fayetteville, NC 28306-9053
☎+1-910-426-5306

Science of the Soul Study Centre
2415 East Washington Street
Petaluma, CA 94954-9274
☎+1-707-762-5082

CARIBBEAN

FOR CARIBBEAN
Mr. Sean Finnigan
R.S.S.B. Foundation
P. O. Box 978, Phillipsburg
St. Maarten, N. A.
☎+599-547-0066

BARBADOS, W.I.
Mrs. Jaya Sabnani
1 Sunset Drive South
Fort George Heights
St. Michael BB111 02

CURACAO, N.A.
Mrs. Reshma Jethmalani
Science of the Soul Study Centre
Kaya Seru di Milon 6-9
Santa Catharina
☎+599-9-747-0226

GRENADA, W.I.
Mr. Prakash Amarnani
P.O. Box 726, St. Georges

GUYANA
Mrs. Indu Lalwani
115, Garnette Street
Newtown Kitty, Georgetown

HAITI, W.I.
Mrs. Mousson Finnigan
P.O. Box 2314
Port-au-Prince

JAMAICA, W.I.
Mrs. Reshma Daswani
17 Colombus Height
First Phase, Ocho Rios

ST. MAARTEN, N.A.
Mr. Haresh Balani
R.S.S.B. Foundation
P. O. Box 978
Phillipsburg
☎+599-547-0066

ST. THOMAS
Mrs. Hema Melwani
P.O. Box 600145
USVI-VI00801-6145

SURINAME
Mr. Chandru Samtani
15 Venus Straat
Paramaribo

TRINIDAD, W.I.
Mr. Chandru Chatlani
20 Admiral Court
Westmoorings-by-Sea, Westmoorings

FOR CENTRAL & SOUTH AMERICA

Mr. Hiro W. Balani
Paseo De Farola, 3, Piso 6
Edificio Marina, Malaga, Spain 29016

CENTRAL AMERICA

BELIZE
Mrs. Milan Bhindu Hotchandani
5789 Goldson Avenue, Belize City

PANAMA
Mr. Ashok Tikamdas Dinani
P.O. Box 0302, 00830 Colon

SOUTH AMERICA

ARGENTINA
Mrs. Estela M.I.
Calle Guemes 249, Acassuso
Buenos Aires 1641

BRAZIL
Mr. Guillerme Almeida
SQN 315, Bloco C, Apto. 306 Brasilia
DF 70-774-030

CHILE
Mr. Vijay Harjani
Pasaje Cuatro No. 3438
Sector Chipana, Iquique

COLOMBIA
Mrs. Emma Orozco
Calle 45, #99-25, Medellin 49744

ECUADOR
Dr. Fernando Flores Villalva
Radha Soami Satsang Beas
Calle Marquez de Varela
OE 3-68y Avda. America
P.O. Box 17-21-115, Quito
☎+5932-2-555-988

PERU
Mr. Carlos Fitts
P.O. Box 18-0658
Lima 18

VENEZUELA
Mrs. Helen Paquin
Radha Soami Satsang Beas
Av. Los Samanes con
Av. Los Naranjos Conj
Res. Florida 335
La Florida, Caracas 1012

EUROPE

AUSTRIA
Mr. Hansjorg Hammerer
Sezenweingasse 10, A-5020 Salzburg

BELGIUM
Mr. Piet J. E. Vosters
Driezenstraat 26, Turnhout 2300

BULGARIA
Mr. Deyan Stoyanov
Foundation Radha Soami Satsang Beas
P. O. Box 39, 8000 Bourgas

CYPRUS
Mr. Heraclis Achilleos
P. O. Box 29077, 1035 Nicosia

CZECH REPUBLIC
Mr. Vladimir Skalsky
Maratkova 916, 142 00 Praha 412

DENMARK
Mr. Tony Sharma
Sven Dalsgaardsvej 33, DK-7430 Ikast

FINLAND
Ms. Anneli Wingfield
P. O. Box 1422, 00101 Helsinki

FRANCE
Mr. Pierre de Proyart
7 Quai Voltaire, Paris 75007

GERMANY
Mr. Rudolf Walberg
P. O. Box 1544, D-65800 Bad Soden

GIBRALTAR
Mr. Sunder Mahtani
RSSB Charitable Trust Gibraltar
15 Rosia Road
☎+350-412-67

GREECE
Mr. Themistoclis Gianopoulos
6 Platonos Str. 17672 Kallithea, Attiki

ITALY
Mrs. Wilma Salvatori Torri
Via Bacchiglione 3, 00199 Rome

*THE NETHERLANDS
(HOLLAND)*
Mr. Henk Keuning
Kleizuwe2, Vreeland 3633AE

Radha Soami Satsang Beas
Middenweg 145 E
1394 AH Nederhorst den Berg
☎+31-294-255-255

NORWAY
Mr. Manoj Kaushal
Langretta 8
N-1279 Oslo

POLAND
Mr. Vinod Sharma
Ul. 1go Sierpnia 36 B, M-100
PL-02-134 Warsaw

PORTUGAL
Mrs. Sharda Lodhia
Torres das Palmeiras, Lote 68, 11º C,
2780-145 Oeiras

ROMANIA
Mrs. Carmen Cismas
C.P. 6-12, 810600 Braila

SLOVENIA
Mr. Marko Bedina
Brezje pri Trzicu 68, 4290 Trzic

SPAIN
Mr. J. W. Balani
Fundacion Cultural RSSB
Fca Loma del Valle S/N
Cruce de Penon de Zapata
Alhaurin De la Torre, Malaga 29130
☎+34-952-414-679

SWEDEN
Mr. Lennart Zachen
Norra Sonnarpsvägen 29
SE-286 72 Asljunga

SWITZERLAND
Mr. Sebastian Züst
Weissenrainstrasse 48
CH 8707 Uetikon am See

UNITED KINGDOM
Mr. Narinder Singh Johal
Haynes Park, Haynes
MK45 3BL Bedford
☎+44-1234-381-234

AFRICA

BENIN
Mr. Jaikumar T. Vaswani
01 Boite Postale 951
Atlantique, Cotonou 01

BOTSWANA
Dr. Krishan Lal Bhateja
P. O. Box 402539, Gaborone

CONGO
Mr. Prahlad Parbhu
143 Kasai Ave. Lubumbashi

GHANA
Mr. Murli Chatani
Radha Soami Satsang Beas
P. O. Box 3976, Accra
☎+233-242-057-309

IVORY COAST
Mr. Konan N'Dri
Boite Postale 569, Abidjan 08

KENYA
Mr. Surinder Singh Ghir
35 Mutty Court
(Kipepu RD), Nairobi

LESOTHO
Mr. Sello Wilson Moseme
P. O. Box 750, Leribe 300

LIBYA (G.S.P.L.A.J.)
Mr. Roshan Lal
P.O. Box 38930, Bani Walid

MADAGASCAR
Mr. Francis Murat
Lote 126B, Ambohiminono
Antanetibe, Antananarivo 101

MAURITIUS
Dr. I. Fagoonee
17 Manick Avenue
La Louise, Quatre Bornes

NAMIBIA
Mrs. Jennifer Carvill
P. O. Box 449
Swakopmund 9000

NIGERIA
Mr. Nanik N. Balani
G.P.O. Box 5054, Marina, Lagos

RÉUNION
Ms. Marie-Lynn Marcel
5 Chemin 'Gonneau, Bernica
St Gillesles Hauts 97435

SIERRA LEONE
Mr. Kishore S. Mahboobani
82/88 Kissy Dock Yard
P. O. Box 369, Freetown

SOUTH AFRICA
Mr. Gordon Clive Wilson
P. O. Box 47182, Greyville 4023

Radha Soami Satsang Beas
P.O. Box 5270, Cresta 2118
☎+27-11-792-7644

SWAZILAND
Mr. Peter Dunseith
P. O. Box 423, Mbabane

TANZANIA
Mr. D.N. Pandit
P.O. Box 1963, Dar-Es-Salaam

UGANDA
Mr. Sylvester Kakooza
Radha Soami Satsang Beas
P. O. Box 31381
Kampala

ZAMBIA
Mr. Chrispin Lwali
P.O. Box 12094
Nchanga North Township
Chingola

ZIMBABWE
Mr. G.D. Wright
Pharmanova, P. O. Box 1726
Harare

MIDDLE EAST

BAHRAIN
Mr. Mangat Rai Rudra
Flat No. 12, Building No. 645
Road No. 2107
Manama 321

ISRAEL
Mr. Michael Yaniv
Moshav Sde Nitzan 59
D.N. Hanegev 85470

KUWAIT
Mr. Vijay Kumar
Yousef AL Badar Street Salmiya
Block 10, Flat #8, Bldg 28

U.A.E.
Mr. Daleep Jatwani
Radha Soami Services Centre
P.O. Box 37816, Dubai
☎+971-4-339-4773

Books on This Science

SOAMI JI MAHARAJ
Sar Bachan Prose (The Yoga of the Sound Current)
Sar Bachan Poetry (Selections)

BABA JAIMAL SINGH
Spiritual Letters

MAHARAJ SAWAN SINGH
The Dawn of Light
Discourses on Sant Mat
My Submission
Philosophy of the Masters, in 5 volumes
Spiritual Gems
Tales of the Mystic East

MAHARAJ JAGAT SINGH
The Science of the Soul
Discourses on Sant Mat, Volume II

MAHARAJ CHARAN SINGH
Die to Live
Divine Light
Light on Saint John
Light on Saint Matthew
Light on Sant Mat
The Master Answers
The Path
Quest for Light
Spiritual Discourses, in 2 volumes
Spiritual Heritage
Thus Saith the Master

BOOKS ABOUT THE MASTERS
Call of the Great Master—Daryai Lal Kapur
Heaven on Earth—Daryai Lal Kapur
Treasure Beyond Measure—Shanti Sethi
With a Great Master in India—Julian P. Johnson
With the Three Masters, in 3 volumes—Rai Sahib Munshi Ram

INTRODUCTION TO SPIRITUALITY
A Spiritual Primer—Hector Esponda Dubin
Honest Living—M. F. Singh

The Inner Voice—C. W. Sanders
Liberation of the Soul—J. Stanley White
Life is Fair: The Law of Cause and Effect—Brian Hines

BOOKS ON MYSTICISM
A Treasury of Mystic Terms, Part I: The Principles of Mysticism (6 volumes)—John Davidson
The Holy Name: Mysticism in Judaism—Miriam Caravella
Yoga and the Bible—Joseph Leeming

BOOKS ON SANT MAT IN GENERAL
In Search of the Way—Flora E. Wood
Living Meditation: A Journey beyond Body and Mind—Hector Esponda Dubin
Message Divine—Shanti Sethi
The Mystic Philosophy of Sant Mat—Peter Fripp
Mysticism: The Spiritual Path, in 2 volumes—Lekh Raj Puri
The Path of the Masters—Julian P. Johnson
Radha Soami Teachings—Lekh Raj Puri

MYSTICS OF THE EAST SERIES
Bulleh Shah—J. R. Puri and T.R. Shangari
Dadu: The Compassionate Mystic—K. N. Upadhyaya
Dariya Sahib: Saint of Bihar—K. N. Upadhyaya
Guru Nanak: His Mystic Teachings—J. R. Puri
Guru Ravidas: The Philosopher's Stone—K. N. Upadhyaya
Kabir: The Great Mystic—Isaac A. Ezekiel
Kabir: The Weaver of God's Name—V. K. Sethi
Mira: The Divine Lover—V. K. Sethi
Saint Namdev—J. R. Puri and V. K. Sethi
Saint Paltu: His life and teachings—Isaac A. Ezekiel
Sarmad: Martyr to Love Divine—Isaac A. Ezekiel
Sultan Bahu—J. R. Puri and K. S. Khak
Tukaram: The Ceaseless Song of Devotion—C. Rajwade
Tulsi Sahib: Saint of Hathras—J. R. Puri and V. K. Sethi

BOOKS FOR CHILDREN
The Journey of the Soul—Victoria Jones

For Internet orders, please visit: www.rssb.org

For book orders <u>within</u> India, please write to:

Radha Soami Satsang Beas
BAV Distribution Centre, 5 Guru Ravi Dass Marg
Pusa Road, New Delhi 110005